TOMB RAIDER

THE OFFICIAL COOKBOOK
AND TRAVEL GUIDE

TOMB RAIDER™

THE OFFICIAL COOKBOOK
AND TRAVEL GUIDE

Recipes by Tara Theoharis

Text by Sebastian Haley and Meagan Marie

INSIGHT
EDITIONS

San Rafael • Los Angeles • London

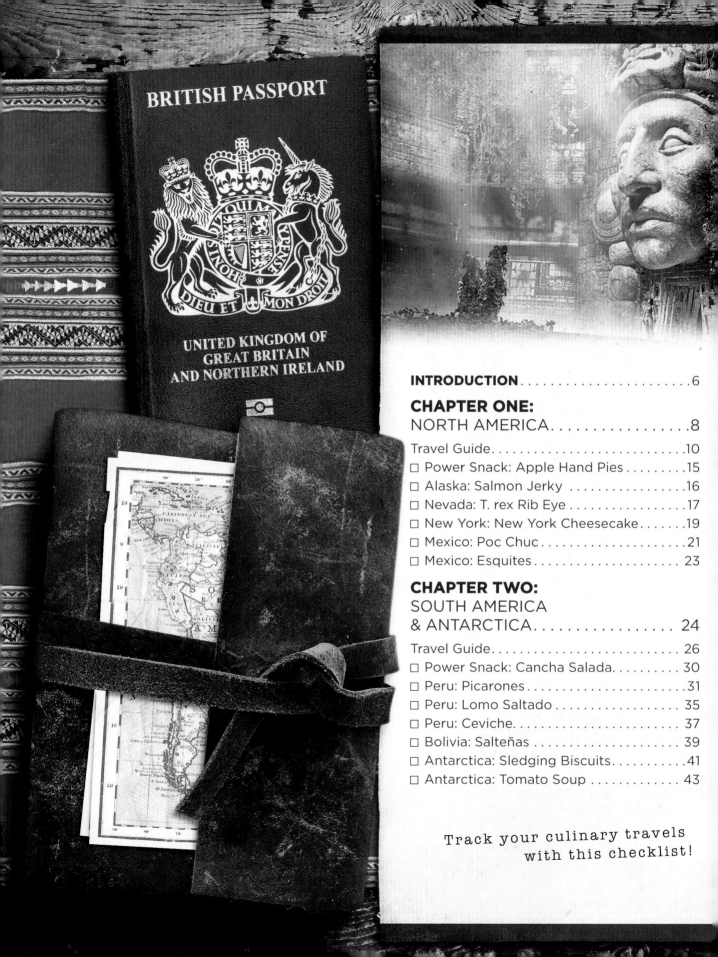

Track your culinary travels
with this checklist!

INTRODUCTION

TARA THEOHARIS
RECIPE DEVELOPER

What does an adventurer eat while traveling around the globe? That was the question I had the privilege of answering while crafting the recipes for this cookbook. I started by envisioning the street food Lara Croft would encounter on her travels—regional food that she could grab on the go, mixed with a few hearty, traditional meals she may enjoy after wrapping up her adventures. I then created a "power snack" for each region, something she could take with her when her expeditions led her away from food sources and something you can enjoy wherever your adventures take you.

The research for these recipes led me to posts written by local bloggers and tourists, and videos of food being made in street carts and restaurants around the world. I watched these professionals make their signature meals and then adapted the recipes so they can be made by a home cook, looking for availability of ingredients in a typical grocery store and finding substitutions for tools and techniques.

After the recipes were written, the fun part began: testing! The recipes were sent to members of the Tomb Raider community in each region, asking them to compare it to the dish they know and love. They gave fantastic feedback, leading to the recipes you see here. This is a love letter to the delicious food that can be found in every corner of the world. I hope you find a new favorite as you explore!

MEAGAN MARIE
COAUTHOR & SENIOR COMMUNITY MANAGER FOR CRYSTAL DYNAMICS

For twenty-five years, Lara Croft has inspired fans, including myself, to expand their horizons and seek adventure. I've been privileged to travel the world as Lara's coworker of sorts, showcasing our work on the Tomb Raider franchise and engaging with our fans across the globe. I have countless wonderful memories from these trips, and the great food, conversations, and company are right up there with seeing ancient ruins, monuments, and natural wonders.

As much as I remember being in awe of the Christ the Redeemer statue in Rio, I also feel absurdly lucky to have been treated to homemade feijoada at the house of our official Brazilian Lara Croft Cosplay Ambassador. Visiting the Great Wall of China left a lasting impression, as did the excitement radiating from our Chinese community each time they suggested a new delicacy to try in Beijing. I now associate ful medames with the Egyptian pyramids and can't help but crave dosa and jalebi when I think of my trip to India and the Taj Mahal.

This is all to say that food is undeniably at the center of culture. The ingredients reflect regional resources, the preparation is passed down as tradition, and the consumption is often a centerpiece for community celebrations. We break bread to make guests feel welcome, to comfort those mourning, and to solidify our social bonds.

With all that in mind, collaborating on a cookbook and a travel guide wasn't something we took on lightly, and at times it was daunting. From the start we planned to collaborate with our network of Official Tomb Raider Fansites and fans across the globe to ensure that the recipes were authentic and cultural details accurate. It was also important for us to use Lara's journey as the foundation for this book, but not let it distract from the history, culture, and traditions that are the true star.

I cannot thank our contributors enough for the time and energy they poured into this project, and I hope reading and cooking from this book brings a bit of their world back home to you.

SEBASTIAN HALEY
COAUTHOR

Writing a travel guide during a pandemic is a bit surreal. The world described in this book seems so very, *very* far away. And yet, it has also been imperative to remember that there is an entire planet out there, filled with ancient vestiges signifying ages long since passed, monumental landforms leading to hidden cities, and traditions that have passed down for hundreds or thousands of years. There is so much more to our world than most of us could ever truly imagine, let alone have the privilege (and time) to experience.

Researching and writing this book taught me more about geography and anthropology than my schooling ever did. One of the reasons I never paid much attention during school—aside from busily drawing dragons and robots in my notebooks—was that these topics can honestly be more than a little disheartening. Colonialism, pollution, racial divides, war, insurmountable hardship, genuine evil and corruption, and the erasure of both nature and culture are prevalent

in virtually every corner of the planet throughout humanity's existence. And while that never seems to change, there is also so much beauty and wonder in the world. There is good trying its best to shine through the bad, and many diverse peoples keep that light alive.

Alongside Meagan and Tara, I did my best to try to represent at least a sliver of that beauty in the food, culture, and locales detailed within these pages. My research included documentaries, translating international cookbooks and encyclopedias, and invaluable feedback from Tomb Raider community members from around the world. I may have also stopped to replay a few Tomb Raider games when I was supposed to be sleeping . . . But I hope that I was able to do even the tiniest bit of justice to the traditions and history touched upon in this book and that just maybe I've kindled a small spark of adventure in anyone reading.

CHAPTER ONE
NORTH AMERICA

◐ **KEY LOCATIONS:** Aleutian Islands, Alaska, US; Las Vegas and Area 51, Nevada, US; New York, New York, US; Cozumel, Mexico; Undisclosed, Southern Mexico

Key Terminology:

■ **Indigenous peoples of the Americas:** The original inhabitants of the Americas prior to the arrival of European colonizers.

■ **Pre-Columbian:** A term used to describe the period prior to European colonization.

■ **Central America:** A geographic region comprised of the seven countries that join the North and South American continents, specifically Belize, Costa Rica, El Salvador, Guatemala, Honduras, Nicaragua, and Panama.

■ **Mesoamerica:** An ethno-cultural region from central Mexico to the north of Costa Rica, defined by the history of the pre-Columbian societies that thrived there. These include the Olmec, Maya, and Aztec, among others.

■ **Latin America:** A geographic region extending from Mexico through Central and South America, comprised of countries that primarily speak Latin-based languages, including Spanish, Portuguese, and French.

■ **Caribbean:** A subregion of the Americas comprised of over 700 islands in the Caribbean Sea, as well as parts of Central and South America that have ethno-cultural ties to the region, such as Belize and Guyana.

■ **Latino/a:** An individual from Latin America, irrespective of the language they speak.

■ **Hispanic:** An individual who speaks Spanish, including individuals from Spain.

The North American continent accounts for over 16 percent of the planet's land area at more than nine and a half million square miles. The United Nations recognizes three distinct areas of North America: Northern America, Central America, and the Caribbean. From a geographic standpoint, it also includes an immense number of islands, including the biggest island in the world: Greenland.

The continent stretches from the arctic down to the equator, providing a vast array of diverse climates and geography. Coastal tropics such as the Bahamas and the US state of Hawaii are some of the most popular vacation destinations in the world. Belize is home to well-preserved Maya Ruins, tropical beaches, and the largest barrier reef in the Northern Hemisphere. Straddling the US/Canadian border, Niagara Falls is a set of waterfalls putting out up to six million cubic feet of water per minute, generating substantial hydroelectric power as well as unprecedented visuals for tens of millions of tourists each year.

The Americas were named after the Italian explorer Amerigo Vespucci and first appeared on a map by German cartographers in 1507, although it had been inhabited long before that. The first humans to reach North America did so by way of the Bering land bridge toward the climax of the Last Glacial Period (115,000–17,000 BCE).

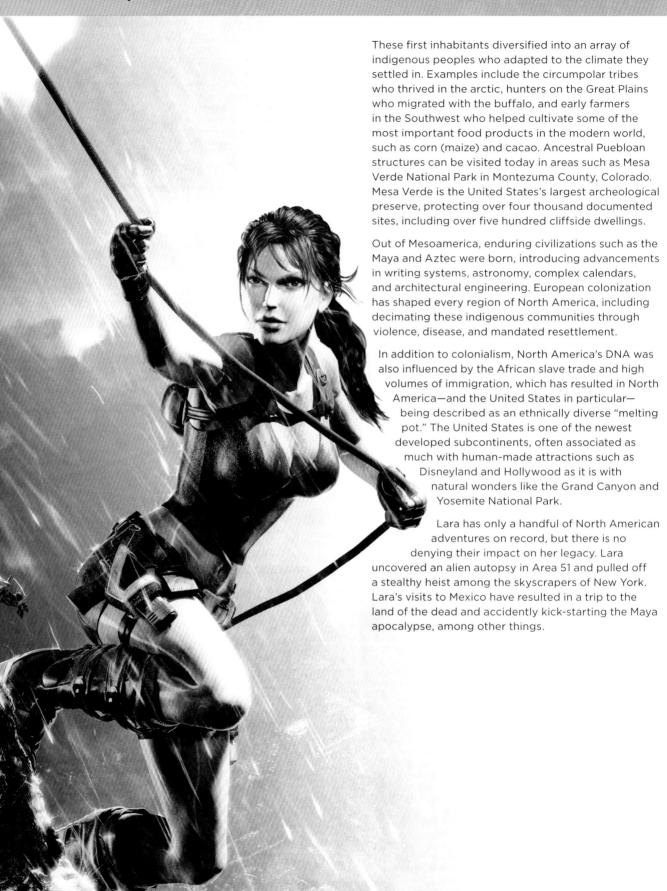

These first inhabitants diversified into an array of indigenous peoples who adapted to the climate they settled in. Examples include the circumpolar tribes who thrived in the arctic, hunters on the Great Plains who migrated with the buffalo, and early farmers in the Southwest who helped cultivate some of the most important food products in the modern world, such as corn (maize) and cacao. Ancestral Puebloan structures can be visited today in areas such as Mesa Verde National Park in Montezuma County, Colorado. Mesa Verde is the United States's largest archeological preserve, protecting over four thousand documented sites, including over five hundred cliffside dwellings.

Out of Mesoamerica, enduring civilizations such as the Maya and Aztec were born, introducing advancements in writing systems, astronomy, complex calendars, and architectural engineering. European colonization has shaped every region of North America, including decimating these indigenous communities through violence, disease, and mandated resettlement.

In addition to colonialism, North America's DNA was also influenced by the African slave trade and high volumes of immigration, which has resulted in North America—and the United States in particular— being described as an ethnically diverse "melting pot." The United States is one of the newest developed subcontinents, often associated as much with human-made attractions such as Disneyland and Hollywood as it is with natural wonders like the Grand Canyon and Yosemite National Park.

Lara has only a handful of North American adventures on record, but there is no denying their impact on her legacy. Lara uncovered an alien autopsy in Area 51 and pulled off a stealthy heist among the skyscrapers of New York. Lara's visits to Mexico have resulted in a trip to the land of the dead and accidently kick-starting the Maya apocalypse, among other things.

ALEUTIAN ISLANDS, ALASKA, US

The breathtaking aurora borealis lights the northern skies over Alaska where Lara spends most of her time in the expanded levels of *Tomb Raider II: Golden Mask* (1999). There she discovers the Furnace of the Gods, an underground river of molten lava, defended by the spirits of Inuit warriors.

Alaska has the largest land area in the United States at approximately 665,000 square miles (17.5 percent of the country), compared to Texas (265,000 square miles) and California (163,000 square miles). For this reason, Alaska is divided into five major regions; Arctic, Interior, Southwest, Southcentral, and Inside Passage. Tourist attractions include glaciers, wildlife sightings, whale watching, crystal-clear rivers, flourishing forests, and snow-covered mountains, to name a few. The awe-inspiring open spaces, crisp air, and welcoming citizens make for a peaceful escape from the overwhelmingly noisy and crowded day-to-day of more urban areas.

The Aleutian Islands are a chain of fourteen large and fifty-five smaller islands; the majority are part of the United States, but some of the most westward islands are under Russian jurisdiction. The native Unangan people—known as the Aleut to outsiders—are settled on both sides of the border. Rife with volcanoes, the islands are the northernmost part of the Pacific Ring of Fire, a tectonically active area that follows the rim of the Pacific Ocean along four continents and is home to regular earthquakes and volcanic eruptions.

Subject to multiple skirmishes during World War II, the Aleutian Islands are the only two sites of significant invasions by enemy forces in the United States since 1812. As part of World War II's Aleutian Islands campaign, Japanese soldiers occupied the islands of Attu and Kiska from 1942 to 1943 before being driven out. Due to this, war memorials are common tourist destinations in the region.

While traveling to Alaska is easy enough by ground, air, or ferry, it's a bit more difficult to get to the remote Aleutian Islands. An estimated 20 percent of flights from Unalaska—the center of the Aleutian Islands population—are canceled due to weather. Alternatively, the Alaska Marine Highway is a no-frills passenger ferry system that services communities with little to no road access to the rest of the state.

LAS VEGAS AND AREA 51, NEVADA, US

For a slightly warmer destination, the desert state of Nevada can reach upwards of 110°F. Lara visits Las Vegas, Nevada, in *Tomb Raider II: Golden Mask* (1999) and the infamous Area 51 in *Tomb Raider III* (1998). Amid the various creatures she encounters in Nevada are T. rexes, orcas, and, naturally, aliens.

Secret government bases notwithstanding, Las Vegas is one of the world's most renowned tourist destinations. A brief three-hour drive from Hollywood, California, the Vegas strip is a showcase of mega-casinos, themed hotels, and extravagant shows that have earned Sin City the title of Entertainment Capital of the World. The five-star buffets offer an endless array of top-shelf international dishes and delicacies. Museums celebrate Las Vegas's dazzling history, while select hotels feature indoor theme parks or waterparks with human-made waves and lazy rivers for visitors of any age.

Among Las Vegas's most elaborate attractions are several miniature global landmarks, such as the Colosseum at Caesars Palace, the Luxor pyramid, the Eiffel Tower at Paris, and the Statue of Liberty at New York-New York. After watching the world-famous dancing fountains in front of the Bellagio, tourists can head to the Fremont Street Experience in Old Vegas. There you can zipline alongside the world's largest video screen, measuring nearly 1,400 feet long, 90 feet wide, and suspended 90 feet above the downtown pedestrian mall.

If you're looking for a desert adventure more in line with Lara's unsanctioned visit to Area 51, there are many off-strip activities to choose between. The Mojave Desert—named after the Mojave tribe indigenous to the area—is the driest desert in the United States. It is mostly situated in California and Nevada, with small portions reaching into Utah and Arizona. Action-inclined Tomb Raider fans would likely enjoy a desert quad bike tour. There are also many on-foot activities available, such as hiking the stunning Arch Rock Nature Trail in Joshua Tree, lodging at Death Valley's Furnace Creek campground, or taking a trip back in time at Petroglyph Canyon in Utah's Zion National Park.

NEW YORK, NEW YORK, US

Tomb Raider: Chronicles (2000) picks up directly after the previous title, *Tomb Raider: The Last Revelation* (1999), with Lara presumed dead. At her memorial, Lara's friends reminisce about several of her past adventures, including a stealth mission to steal a valuable relic in New York.

The City That Never Sleeps is about as big and bustling as they come. With over 8.3 million residents, New York City is the most densely populated major city in the United States. The Statue of Liberty is much farther away (and smaller) than movies have likely led you to believe, but Times Square is exactly as flashy and exciting as it is depicted, with no small assortment of pizzerias, theaters, and subway stations in any given direction.

For a quieter getaway, Central Park spans 843 acres of Manhattan, one of New York's five boroughs. The biologically diverse national landmark features multiple lakes, approximately twenty thousand trees, and hundreds of unique species of animals in addition to those living at the Central Park Zoo. Aside from being one of the state's major tourist attractions, Central Park is commonly used for film shoots, marriage ceremonies, exercise classes, and other events and celebrations.

For those who prefer picturesque scenery safely tucked behind a glass case, New York is home to several notable museums: the Metropolitan Museum of Art, the largest art museum in the United States and one of the largest in the world; the Museum of Modern Art, a highly influential museum focusing on contemporary art such as architecture, photography, film, and digital media; and the American Museum of Natural History, which consists of twenty-six interconnected buildings exhibiting over thirty-four million specimens of animals, plants, minerals, and cultural artifacts.

UNDISCLOSED, SOUTHERN MEXICO

Lara visits Southern Mexico in search of the Maya land of the dead in *Tomb Raider: Underworld* (2008). During this adventure, Lara faces giant spiders and jaguar thralls in her quest to open the gate to the underworld, also known as Xibalba.

Ancient Maya believed cenotes—natural sinkholes that expose the water beneath the ground—led to Xibalba. This would likely bring Lara to the Yucatán Peninsula, which hides many spectacular Maya cultural sites. Among the most well-known are the pristine ancient Maya city-state of Palenque, the ancient city of Coba, tucked deep in the jungle of the state of Quintana Roo; and the Temple of Kukulcán in the great city of Chichen Itza.

Chichen Itza means "at the mouth of the well of the Itza," with the Itza being the politically dominant people of the era. The site sees over two million tourists every year. Not only was it one of the largest cities in the Maya civilization, but also one of the most diverse, as represented by its various architectural styles. An elaborate network of paved causeways connects the many stone buildings, which were originally quite colorful but have since faded considerably.

The Great Ball Court is the largest and most well-preserved ancient ball court in all of Mesoamerica. Measuring 551 by 230 feet, it is roughly five times the size of a professional NBA basketball court. Although the full rules of the ancient sport played here remain a mystery, it is believed that human sacrifice was sometimes involved.

Among the many other points of interest at Chichen Itza are the Temple of Warriors, a towering, stepped pyramid surrounded by rows of columns featuring carvings depicting ancient warriors, and the Sacred Cenote. Known as the Well of Sacrifice, the site was a place of Maya pilgrimage, and thousands of items have been recovered from the bottom of the cenote by archeologists, including gold, rubber, pottery, and human remains.

COZUMEL, MEXICO

Lara uses the Día de los Muertos (Day of the Dead) celebrations to infiltrate ruins guarded by Trinity soldiers at the beginning of *Shadow of the Tomb Raider* (2018). After passing through the Trinity dig site, Lara comes upon an artifact hidden in a Maya temple, and in removing it unwittingly commences the apocalypse.

Visiting the island of Cozumel is much easier for anyone not being hunted by a fictitious mercenary group. Located off the Yucatán Peninsula coast in the Caribbean Sea, Cozumel is a popular tourist destination due to its beautiful sights, endemic wildlife, Maya ruins, and hidden cenotes. Cozumel is also home to two of Mexico's largest annual celebrations—the Cozumel Carnival and the Festival of Santa Cruz and El Cedral Fair—as well as one of many places throughout the country where the Day of the Dead is observed.

The Mexican holiday is celebrated on the first two days of November and involves loved ones gathering to remember and pray for those who have passed on at beautiful and ornate alters called ofrendas. Travelers from around the world come to celebrate Día de los Muertos, though those seeking to experience it in its native country should remain mindful of traditions and be respectful of those communing with their departed loved ones. Tourists should pass on the traditional skull-like face paint unless asked to participate, and supporting local vendors is encouraged as a way to give back to the community hosting the festival.

Thank you to our North American travel guide and recipe consultants: Juan de Jesus Treviño Paz of The New Tomb Raider Collection; Roni Theoharis

NORTH AMERICAN CUISINE
APPLE HAND PIES

| **LOCATION:** NORTH AMERICA | **YIELD:** 8 PIES | **DIFFICULTY RATING:** 1 OUT OF 3 |

Much simpler to transport than a traditional slice of apple pie, these hand pies are a great power snack when you're on the go, giving a quick boost of energy. That being said, if you are eating them from the comfort of your own kitchen, a scoop of vanilla ice cream takes this treat to the next level.

PREP TIME: 5 MINUTES   **COOK TIME:** 40 MINUTES   **INACTIVE TIME:** 30 MINUTES

TOOLS NEEDED: Medium pot, Parchment paper–lined baking sheet

INGREDIENTS:

4 tablespoons (¼ cup) unsalted butter

4 Granny Smith apples, peeled, cored, and diced

½ cup light brown sugar, packed

1 teaspoon ground cinnamon

½ teaspoon kosher salt

1 tablespoon lemon juice

All-purpose flour, for dusting the surface

2 puff pastry sheets, thawed

1 egg, beaten

4 teaspoons sanding sugar

DIRECTIONS:

1. Melt the butter in a medium pot over medium heat, then add the apples, brown sugar, cinnamon, salt, and lemon juice, stirring to combine. Bring to a simmer and cook for 8 minutes or until the apples are soft and the liquid has reduced. Move to a bowl and chill in the refrigerator for at least 30 minutes.

2. On a floured surface, roll each pastry sheet out to a 12-inch square and cut each pastry sheet into 8 equal-sized rectangles, approximately 6 inches by 3 inches. You will have 16 rectangles total.

3. Spoon 3 tablespoons of apple mixture into the center of 8 of the rectangles, leaving a ¼-inch border empty around the entire rectangle.

4. Place the unused rectangles directly on top of the filled rectangles.

5. Using a fork, crimp along the edges until each rectangle is fully sealed. Cut three slits into the top center of each pie. Chill the pies in the fridge for 15 minutes.

6. Preheat the oven to 400°F. Prepare a baking sheet by lining with parchment paper.

7. Place the pies on the prepared baking sheet. Brush the tops of the pies with the beaten egg, and sprinkle each pie with ½ teaspoon of sanding sugar.

8. Bake for 20 to 25 minutes or until puffed up and golden brown.

NORTH AMERICAN CUISINE
SALMON JERKY

LOCATION: ALEUTIAN ISLANDS, ALASKA | **YIELD:** 4 SERVINGS | **DIFFICULTY RATING:** 1 OUT OF 3

Salmon jerky is made by curing salmon with seasonings or juices and then dehydrating the meat. This process makes it difficult for bacteria to penetrate the food's outer surface, providing a long shelf life perfect for snacks and traveling.

RECIPE ORIGINS

Some variation of salmon jerky has been prevalent for many different peoples throughout the ages. The simple process of curing and smoking fish, and the abundance of salmon, enabled everyone from indigenous Americans to ancient Greeks and Romans to document a history with the dish.

PREP TIME: 7 HOURS

COOK TIME: 9 HOURS

TOOLS NEEDED: Large bowl or zippered plastic bag, for marinating, Cooling rack, Baking sheet

INGREDIENTS:

1 pound Alaskan salmon

½ cup soy sauce

1 tablespoon light brown sugar, packed

1 tablespoon lemon juice

2 teaspoons black pepper

1 teaspoon liquid smoke

DIRECTIONS:

1. Remove the pin bones from the salmon, but keep the skin on. This will help keep the salmon together.

2. Freeze the salmon for 1 hour. This will make it easier to cut.

3. Remove the salmon from the freezer and cut it into thin strips, about ¼- to ½-inch-thick lengthwise.

4. Place the salmon in a large bowl or plastic bag and cover with the soy sauce, brown sugar, lemon juice, black pepper, and liquid smoke. Marinate in the refrigerator overnight or for at least 6 hours.

5. Preheat the oven to 150°F, or the lowest temperature it will go. Prepare a baking sheet by placing an oven-safe rack inside.

6. Drain the salmon and pat dry with a paper towel. Place the strips on the prepared baking sheet, and carefully place it in the oven.

7. Dehydrate on the lowest setting of the oven for 9 hours or until dry and chewy. Note: The thicker your salmon, the longer this may take.

8. Remove the skin from the jerky before eating.

LOCATION FEATURED IN:
Tomb Raider II: Golden Mask (1999)

KEY LOCATION:
Melnikov Island (Aleutian Islands)

ESSENTIAL EQUIPMENT:
Snowmobile

T. REX RIB EYE

LOCATION: LAS VEGAS, NEVADA	**YIELD:** 1 LARGE STEAK	**DIFFICULTY RATING:** 1 OUT OF 3

Don't let Lara's nightmarish encounter with a T. rex in Tomb Raider II: Golden Mask *(1999) turn you away from a fierce steak seared and cooked to perfection. This beastly steak is large enough to be from the mighty T. rex itself and would be at home on any Vegas steakhouse menu. Pair it with an herbaceous compound butter for a delicious entrée.*

RECIPE ORIGINS

The word "steak" originates from the fifteenth-century Scandinavian word "steik." Beefsteak and its many variants, including bison, ostrich, camel, and shark, are some of the most popular and sought-after meat dishes around the world. In the United States, steakhouse restaurants are standard among fine-dining establishments and destinations, with over two dozen along the Las Vegas strip alone.

PREP TIME: 100 MINUTES   **COOK TIME:** 10 MINUTES   **INACTIVE TIME:** 10 MINUTES

TOOLS NEEDED: Wire rack, Baking sheet, Small bowl, Plastic wrap, Cast-iron skillet (or other heavy skillet), Meat thermometer

INGREDIENTS:

STEAK:

1 (1½-pound) 1½-inch-thick bone-in rib eye steak

½ tablespoon kosher salt

2 teaspoons rosemary

1 teaspoon black pepper

2 tablespoons olive oil

2 tablespoons salted butter, cut into small chunks

2 cloves garlic

COMPOUND BUTTER:

4 tablespoons (¼ cup) unsalted butter, softened

1 tablespoon minced parsley

½ tablespoon minced chives

Pinch of kosher salt

LOCATION FEATURED IN:
Tomb Raider II: Golden Mask (1999)

KEY LOCATION:
Three Kings Convention

MEMORABLE MOMENT:
Encountering the King of Dinosaurs

DIRECTIONS:

1. Sprinkle the kosher salt over both sides of the steak. Place the steak on a wire rack on top of a baking sheet, and place in the refrigerator for at least 1 hour and up to 3 days.

2. Make the compound butter: Mix together the butter, parsley, chives, and salt in a small bowl. Transfer the compound butter to a sheet of plastic wrap, and roll it up into a log shape. Refrigerate for 1 hour or until firm.

3. Remove the steak from the refrigerator 30 minutes before cooking and let it come to room temperature. Sprinkle both sides with rosemary and black pepper.

4. Heat the olive oil in a medium skillet over high heat.

5. Place the steak on the skillet, and don't move it, allowing it to sear to the pan. Add the salted butter and garlic cloves. Cook for 5 minutes.

6. Turn the steak over and cook for another 5 minutes. While it's cooking, tilt the skillet toward you, allowing the melted butter to pool up. Use a spoon to move that butter up and over the steak, continuously basting it with the butter.

7. Use a meat thermometer to check how done your steak is.

Rare	120°F – 130°F
Medium Rare	130°F – 140°F
Medium	140°F – 150°F
Medium Well	150°F – 160°F

If it's not cooked well enough, cook for another minute and check the temperature again.

8. Remove the steak from the pan and rest on a cutting board for 10 minutes.

9. Slice and serve with a pat of compound butter on top.

NORTH AMERICAN CUISINE
NEW YORK CHEESECAKE

| **LOCATION:** NEW YORK, NEW YORK | **YIELD:** ONE 9-INCH CHEESECAKE | **DIFFICULTY RATING:** 3 OUT OF 3 |

Cream cheese is the key to a good cheesecake. Of all the different preparations for cheesecake, New York cheesecake is of note due to American cream cheese being developed in 1872 by William Lawrence of Chester, New York. Lawrence was attempting to re-create French Neufchâtel cheese and accidentally invented a softer and surprisingly richer reduced-fat variant.

New York cheesecake is profoundly decadent, with a rich and creamy consistency. Sour cream is sometimes added in place of heavy cream, as it preserves the cheesecake's texture and flavor better when being frozen, as is the case with this particular recipe.

RECIPE ORIGINS

Cheesecake is believed to originate from ancient Greece, where it was served to athletes of the first-ever Olympic Games in 776 BCE. This recipe, however, did not resemble modern cheesecake and was more akin to a boiled pudding.

PREP TIME: 10 MINUTES   **COOK TIME:** 2 HOURS   **INACTIVE TIME:** 5 HOURS

TOOLS NEEDED: 9-inch springform pan, Stand mixer, Heavy-duty aluminum foil, Roasting pan or large casserole dish, Small pot, Mesh strainer

INGREDIENTS:

CRUST:

15 graham crackers, broken down into fine crumbs

⅓ cup unsalted butter, melted

3 tablespoons granulated sugar

Pinch of kosher salt

FILLING:

6 cups boiling water

32 ounces cream cheese, room temperature

2 cups granulated sugar

2 tablespoons cornstarch

1 teaspoon vanilla extract

1 teaspoon lemon zest

2 teaspoons lemon juice

¼ teaspoon kosher salt

5 eggs and 1 egg yolk, room temperature

½ cup sour cream, room temperature

TOPPING:

2 cups raspberries

¼ cup granulated sugar

2 teaspoons lemon juice

2 teaspoons cornstarch

1 tablespoon cold water

½ teaspoon vanilla extract

Additional fresh raspberries, for garnish

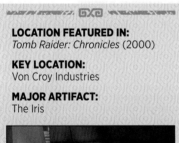

LOCATION FEATURED IN:
Tomb Raider: Chronicles (2000)

KEY LOCATION:
Von Croy Industries

MAJOR ARTIFACT:
The Iris

Continued on page 20

Continued from page 19

DIRECTIONS:

1. Preheat the oven to 350°F and grease the bottom and sides of a 9-inch springform pan. Set aside.

2. In a medium mixing bowl, mix together the graham cracker crumbs, melted butter, sugar, and salt. Press the mixture evenly into the bottom of the pan and halfway up the sides.

3. Bake the crust for 12 minutes, or until golden brown and set. Let cool.

4. Reduce the oven temperature to 325°F. Bring 6 cups of water to a boil.

5. Place the cream cheese in a mixing bowl, and mix on medium until smooth. Reduce the speed to low, and slowly add the sugar and cornstarch. Mix for 2 minutes, or until light and fluffy. Using a spatula, scrape down the sides of the bowl. Add the vanilla, lemon zest, lemon juice, and salt, and mix for another minute.

6. Add the eggs, one at a time, and the egg yolk, mixing fully between each addition. Scrape down the sides of the bowl, then add the sour cream. Mix until combined.

7. Put the cooled springform pan onto three large layers of heavy-duty aluminum foil, and bring each layer of foil up along the sides of the pan, so no boiling water, when poured, can seep in. Pour the cheesecake mixture into the pan until it almost reaches the top. Carefully place the pan in a large roasting pan or casserole dish, and put on the center rack of the oven.

8. Pour the boiling water into the roasting pan, allowing it to come halfway up the sides of the springform pan.

9. Bake the cheesecake for 90 minutes without opening the oven or disturbing it in any way. At this point, the cheesecake should be relatively firm along the edges but still wobbly in the center. Turn off the oven and leave the cheesecake in there, with the door cracked open, for one hour.

10. Remove the springform pan from the water bath and remove the aluminum foil. Run a knife along the edge of the pan to loosen the cheesecake sides from the walls. Cover with plastic wrap and transfer to the refrigerator. Let cool for at least 4 hours.

11. Make the raspberry sauce for the top: Place raspberries, sugar, and lemon juice in a small pot over medium heat. Bring to a boil and cook for 9 minutes, breaking down the raspberries as they soften and begin releasing their juices. Mix the cornstarch and the cold water together, and then add the cornstarch mixture and the vanilla extract to the raspberry mixture. Mix and allow to cook for 1 additional minute, or until the sauce has thickened.

12. Strain the sauce through a mesh strainer.

13. Remove the sides of the springform pan. Spoon some raspberry sauce over the top and garnish with additional fresh raspberries. When ready to serve, slice into the cold cheesecake with a hot knife.

POC CHUC

| **LOCATION:** COZUMEL, MEXICO | **YIELD:** 4 SERVINGS | **DIFFICULTY RATING:** 1 OUT OF 3 |

Poc chuc is a pork dish marinated in citrus and charred on an open grill. Typical sides include rice, beans, pickled onion, fresh avocado, and tortillas.

Using a molcajete is a foundational part of cooking Mexican food even when traditional blenders or food processors are available—it is said to create higher quality and more flavorful dishes. The tool's name comes from the Nahuatl word "mollocaxtli," which refers to a concave stone used for making sauce. The tool can be traced back over six thousand years in Mesoamerica.

RECIPE ORIGINS

Poc chuc is derived from the Mayan words "poc" (toast) and "chuc" (charcoal). Although poc chuc is a signature dish of the Yucatán, its origins are still debated, as some of its elements, including pork, did not exist in pre-Columbian Yucatán.

PREP TIME: 65 MINUTES   **COOK TIME:** 10 MINUTES

TOOLS NEEDED: Large bowl or bag for marinating, Grill or large pan, Molcajete or mortar and pestle (or food processor)

INGREDIENTS:

POC CHUC:

1 pound boneless pork chops

¾ cup sour orange juice (or ½ cup orange juice and ¼ cup lime juice)

2 cloves garlic, minced

1 teaspoon sea salt

½ teaspoon oregano

Tortillas, for serving

CHILTOMATE SALSA:

6 Roma tomatoes

1 white onion, cut in half

1 habanero pepper

1 teaspoon salt

1 teaspoon cilantro, chopped

DIRECTIONS:

1. Pound the pork chops thin with a meat tenderizer. Place in a large bowl or bag with the orange juice, garlic, salt, and oregano. Let everything marinate in the refrigerator for at least 1 hour, or up to overnight.

2. Make the chiltomate salsa: Char the tomatoes, the onion halves, and pepper on a grill or a pan with a tablespoon of oil over high heat. Cut off the tops of the pepper (and deseed for a milder salsa). Place the charred tomatoes and pepper into a molcajete and grind until a chunky salsa forms, about 2 minutes. Move to a larger bowl. Dice the charred onion and add to the bowl. Mix in the salt and cilantro. Set aside.

3. Take the marinated pork and place on a grill over medium-high heat or a large pan over high heat and cook for 1 minute on each side, or until it browns/shows grill marks and is fully cooked.

4. Serve the pork with a spoonful of the chiltomate salsa on top and tortillas on the side.

LOCATION FEATURED IN:
Shadow of the Tomb Raider (2018)

KEY LOCATION:
Día de los Muertos Celebration

MAJOR ARTIFACT:
Key of Chak Chel

NORTH AMERICAN CUISINE
ESQUITES

| **LOCATION:** UNDISCLOSED, SOUTHERN MEXICO | **YIELD:** 4 SERVINGS | **DIFFICULTY RATING:** 1 OUT OF 3 |

Esquites, also known as "elote en vaso" (corn in a cup), is a popular Mexican snack sold by street vendors and small markets. Esquites is made from corn sautéed in butter. It is served in snack-sized cups with various toppings, such as salt, lime juice, hot sauce, mayonnaise, and chili powder. The spicy snack is known in many other countries simply as "Mexican corn."

RECIPE ORIGINS

The word "esquites" originates from "ízquitl," the Nahuatl word for "toasted corn." Nahuatl, or Mexicano, is a group of Uto-Aztecan languages spoken by roughly 1.7 million people primarily living in Central Mexico and dating back to the seventh century CE.

PREP TIME: 10 MINUTES

COOK TIME: 10 MINUTES

TOOLS NEEDED: Large skillet

INGREDIENTS:

2 tablespoons salted butter

2 to 3 cups of fresh/raw corn kernels (sliced off of 4 ears of corn)

½ teaspoon kosher salt

1 clove garlic, minced

1 jalapeño, seeded and diced

⅛ teaspoon cayenne pepper

¼ teaspoon chili powder

2 tablespoons mayonnaise

2 tablespoons cotija cheese

2 tablespoons cilantro, chopped

1 lime, cut into 4 wedges

DIRECTIONS:

1. Melt the butter in a large skillet on high heat, then add the corn kernels. Sprinkle with kosher salt and don't move the corn kernels for 2 minutes, allowing them to char. Mix, and then cook for another 2 minutes. Continue this two more times for a total cook time of 8 minutes.

2. Let the corn cool slightly, and transfer to a large bowl. Mix in the garlic, jalapeño, cayenne pepper, chili powder, mayonnaise, cotija, and cilantro.

3. Scoop the mixture into four small cups or bowls and serve with a lime wedge.

LOCATION FEATURED IN:
Tomb Raider: Underworld (2008)

KEY LOCATION:
Xibalba

MAJOR ARTIFACT:
Thor's Belt

CHAPTER TWO
SOUTH AMERICA & ANTARCTICA

◑ **KEY LOCATIONS:** Vilcabamba and El Paraíso, Peru; Peruvian Amazonia; Tiwanaku, Bolivia; Undisclosed, Antarctica

Key Terminology:

Please reference page 8 for more important terminology related to the Americas.

■ **Antarctic Circle:** The most southernly circle of latitude on maps of Earth, and home to the Antarctic region. Nearly all of the continent of Antarctica is in the Antarctic circle, and the only inhabitants are those of research stations by countries who are a part of the Antarctic Treaty.

■ **Cradle of Civilization:** A term used to describe geographic locations where civilizations are thought to have independently emerged. Academically accepted Cradles of Civilization include the Fertile Crescent—birthing both Mesopotamia and Ancient Egypt—the North Indian River Plain, North China Plain, Mesoamerica's Gulf Coast, and the Andean Coast.

South America is one of the most biodiverse destinations in the world and a continent of extremes. It is home to both the Andes Mountains, the longest continental mountain range on the planet, and the Amazon River, one of the longest rivers in the world. The Amazon River and its many tributaries form the Amazon Rainforest, the world's largest rainforest and home to an unimaginable number of plant and animal species.

The extremes continue: Venezuela's Angel Falls is the highest uninterrupted waterfall in the world; Lake Titicaca, straddling the border between Bolivia and Peru, is the highest navigable lake in the world; and Chile's Atacama Desert is the driest place on Earth outside the North and South Poles. Encompassing the entire tip of South America, Patagonia offers travelers the chance to traverse desert steppes, visit fjords, and climb glaciers. And this is all just found on the mainland continent—there is so much more to explore in the Southern Caribbean, the Galápagos Islands, and beyond.

In addition to its natural beauty, South America also has an extensive history of vibrant indigenous cultures and is home to some of the most stunning archeological sites in the world. The Norte Chico civilization (also known as the Caral Civilization) is considered one of several cradles of civilization and is the oldest in the Americas, thriving in the same period of the first dynasty in Egypt. Although they lived in a preceramic culture, their earthwork mounds and plazas are known worldwide. The Nazca culture emerged sometime around 100 BCE and left behind a stunning array of textiles, ceramics, and most uniquely their geoglyphs—the Nazca Lines best viewed from high above the ground. The Inca Empire emerged in the thirteenth century and grew to be the largest empire in pre-Columbian America, spanning much of the Western continent before the beginning of Spanish rule.

Although colonialism and slavery left an indelible mark on South America, the continent's indigenous history is preserved through archaeology, anthropology, and living descendants; an estimated thirty million+ people identify as indigenous South Americans today. While most of South America speaks Spanish, followed by Portuguese, Quechua—the main language family of the Inca Empire—and its variants are still spoken by millions of people today.

Some of Lara's greatest adventures begin in South America (*Tomb Raider* (1996), *Tomb Raider: Legend* (2006)), where the continent's rich ancient history and endless hidden treasures make for the perfect virtual playground. The apocalyptic events of *Shadow of the Tomb Raider* (2018) occur almost entirely in South America, and who could forget fighting a mad-scientist-turned-alien-spider deep within the Antarctic in the climactic finale of *Tomb Raider III* (1998)?

VILCABAMBA, PERU

The Lost City of the Incas is undoubtedly one of the most memorable locations in Tomb Raider history, as it marks the opening levels of both *Tomb Raider* (1996) and *Tomb Raider: Anniversary* (2007). The danger and wonders are endless as Lara first encounters wild wolves and bears, navigates through beautiful landscapes and deadly traps, and makes her way to The Lost Valley for a showdown with several raptors and a T. rex.

In 1539, what was left of the Inca Empire retreated from Spanish rule into the remote jungles of Vilcabamba and established their new capital. They existed peacefully for forty years, until their stronghold eventually fell. The jungle reclaimed Vilcabamba, and its exact location was lost to time, until three Peruvian residents from Cusco rediscovered it in the 1890s, naming it Espiritu Pampa (Plain of the Spirits). The American explorer Hiram Bingham famously launched several expeditions to Peru in search of the lost capital after the turn of the twentieth century. Guided by locals, he visited Vilcabamba but didn't realize it was in fact the Lost City of the Incas. He had brought Machu Picchu to international attention in 1911 and believed it to be the final Incan stronghold. Vilcabamba was not correctly identified as the capital until the 1960s. Interestingly, artifacts belonging to the Wari civilization have been discovered in the ruins of Vilcabamba in the past decade, indicating that the site had been populated millennia before it became the Inca capital.

While you can visit Vilcabamba, it is inaccessible by vehicles. An array of guided hikes are available; the shortest is estimated at nine hours if you travel by vehicle as far as allowed. Other guided hikes start from Cusco, if you're up for a five-day adventure through mountains and jungles. Because it is so far off the beaten path, those who make the trek to Vilcabamba enjoy the ancient city with few other tourists around.

Vilcabamba was one of four major Inca settlements in the region, which also includes Choquequirao, Vitcos, and Machu Picchu. Unlike Vilcabamba, Machu Picchu was not destroyed during the Spanish conquest and remained hidden from the outside world for centuries, making it one of the most well-preserved examples of Inca architecture. Now a UNESCO World Heritage Site, Machu Picchu has over 1.4 million visitors each year, deeming it Peru's most visited tourist attraction. A great deal of effort has been made toward sustainable tourism to help protect and maintain the ancient site, which includes limiting regular access.

With that in mind, planning ahead to visit Machu Picchu is a necessity. There are two suggested ways to visit. The first is to hike the Inca Trail, a small part of an extensive network of trails that once united the empire, which requires booking with an agency months in advance. It is an arduous twenty-six-mile hike at high altitude—over thirteen thousand feet at the highest point—so getting acclimatized in Cusco first is recommended and a medical checkup is required before you depart. Most Inca Trail tours last four days and three nights and can allow you to reach the ruins before the mass of tour buses arrive. Plus, the journey itself boasts phenomenal views.

The second and more common way is to take the train from Cusco to Aguas Calientes, which is a four-hour ride with a beautiful view of the Sacred Valley of the Incas, and then bus or walk the rest of the way to the ruins, though this may result in a more crowded experience with limited site access.

EL PARAÍSO, PERU

Lara Croft and her longtime friend Amanda Evert explore the archaeological excavation site of El Paraíso in *Tomb Raider: Legend* (2006), shortly before tragedy befalls Amanda and the two are fated to become enemies. Lara returns to the site many years later to unravel the mysteries behind Amanda's alleged death.

Located near Peru's capital of Lima, El Paraíso, which translates to "The Paradise," is a preceramic settlement founded roughly four thousand years ago, and the massive site spreads across more than 130 acres. Surrounded by agricultural land, it is a place of ongoing archeological research. The focal points of the site are nearly a dozen pre-Inca step pyramids, reinforcing the common belief that rather than it being a residential area, it was an economic hub or religious gathering center. In addition to these structures, excavations have surfaced textile remnants, wood and bone artifacts, and other everyday items such as ancient knitting tools and a mirror.

In 2013, remains of a temple were discovered in the site's main pyramid. That same year, property developers illegally bulldozed one of El Paraíso's pyramids. Strict protection protocols have been put in place, as much of El Paraíso remains to be excavated. As these structures are uncovered, they will provide more insight into everyday life and the storied history of ancient Peru.

While El Paraíso is an active excavation, there are tours available to visit it and other ruins in the Callao region. We also suggest you visit the UNESCO World Heritage Site of Caral several hours outside of Lima. Often noted as the most ancient city in the Americas—although new sites are still being uncovered to this day—Caral is one of the largest Norte Chico sites ever uncovered.

Stopping by some of the fantastic museums in Lima is also highly recommended. The National Museum of the Archaeology, Anthropology, and History of Peru is at the top of the list, which covers the entire history of human-occupied Peru with over one hundred thousand artifacts.

PERUVIAN AMAZONIA

Shadow of the Tomb Raider (2018) sees Lara exploring the vast Peruvian jungle, also known as Peruvian Amazonia. Hunted by mercenaries and jaguars alike, Lara proves herself to be the apex predator as she makes her way to Hidden City of Paititi.

Peru's portion of the Amazon rainforest is second in size only to Brazil's and is broken into two segments: the warmer lowland jungles and cooler highland jungles, which border the Andes. While the Peruvian jungle accounts for more than half of the country's land, it is home to only a tiny percentage of the population,

estimated to be 5 percent. The population includes various indigenous cultures such as the Aguaruna and Urarina people; some of many tribes are considered "uncontacted" and live in nearly total isolation from the outside world. There are some major cities in the region, however, the largest being Iquitos, known as the capital of the Peruvian Amazon. You can reach Iquitos only by air or water—it isn't accessible by road.

A short two-hour flight from Lima will bring you to Puerto Maldonado, a great place to focus your Amazon adventure since it is considered the biodiversity capital of Peru. Once there you can home in on the level of adventure you're up for, though tourists of all skill levels can't go wrong with a canopy walk along the Madre de Dios River. Activity options are endless, from piranha fishing to nighttime river cruises to volunteering at the Amazon shelter rescue and rehabilitation center. The Mariposario Tambopata butterfly farm lets you walk among hundreds of the Amazon's most stunning species. Monkey Island is also a fantastic choice, letting you see eight different varieties of monkeys and other wildlife as they are being rehabilitated for release back into the jungle. If you're up for it, rafting along the Tambopata River provides serene experiences for beginners or white-water options for adrenaline junkies.

Efforts to protect the Peruvian Amazon from illegal logging, gold mining, and oil drilling have increased over the last few decades, as all are a risk to both the natural resources and indigenous people of the area.

TIWANAKU, BOLIVIA

Bolivia helped usher in a new generation of Tomb Raider titles, serving as the opening and ending levels of *Tomb Raider: Legend* (2006). Players were introduced to Crystal Dynamics' Lara Croft as she ascended to explore the beautiful Bolivian ruins of Tiwanaku, intentionally doing so without proper climbing gear for the added thrill.

If you're eager to check out the real-world Tiwanaku, be sure to stop by the treasured Lake Titicaca on your way south. The massive lake is shared between Peru and Bolivia, and is believed to be the birthplace of the Inca Empire. The resort town of Copacabana is so famous you've likely heard at least one song about it, and travelers can take boat trips to Isla del Sol to explore ancient Inca ruins. The island is still occupied by more than eight hundred indigenous families who farm, fish, and augment income with tourism. Plan on a day-trip at a minimum to explore the island. It takes three hours to trek across Isla del Sol, but with more than eighty ruins to see you'll want to take your time. Remember that Lake Titicaca is at high elevation, so pace yourself with the hiking.

While Lake Titicaca was an important place for the Inca Empire, it is believed that other earlier cultures also lived on the lake, including the people of Tiwanaku. To see remnants of their capital, travel south to the Tiwanaku UNESCO World Heritage Site. It is a stunning example of pre-Columbian architectural structures, as well as one of the largest historical sites in South America. It is not quite what you'd expect after playing *Tomb Raider: Legend* (2006), however.

In *Legend*, Lara ascends a lush mountain side with waterfalls in a climate instead similar to the Yungas forest near La Paz. Tiwanaku is an arid, cold environment with little vegetation, but like in the game, it does boast an impressive pyramid. Tiwanaku is notable not only for its advanced agricultural technology and perfectly carved stones with ninety-degree angles—defying the limitations of the era's tools—but also for its unfinished buildings. The seemingly overnight disappearance of the inhabitants remains a mystery.

ANTARCTICA

To explorers and historians, Antarctica is notable for many reasons, including being the last discovered continent in recorded history. No one country has a claim to Antarctica. Rather, the continent is governed by the innovative Antarctic Treaty. Established in 1959, the Antarctic Treaty is an emblem of international cooperation and establishes enforced principles over the region. An emphasis is placed on freedom of scientific investigation and non-militarization of the continent and the surrounding ocean. There are an estimated five thousand scientific personnel spread across over sixty national research facilities during peak summer months, but as few as one thousand remain during the winter. Over forty-five thousand tourists visit Antarctica each year.

In *Tomb Raider III* (1998) Lara Croft follows a trail of extraterrestrial artifacts littered across the world. Eventually these artifacts point her to Antarctica, where she uncovers a massive meteorite cavern. Interestingly, the majority of meteorites found in the world *are* collected in Antarctica, for a variety of reasons. Most notably, their dark colors clearly contrast against the ice and snow, which doesn't usually feature naturally occurring rocks. Also, the desert-like conditions of Antarctica keep the rocks from eroding as they do in other parts of the world. When conditions are right and the top layer of massive ice sheets evaporate, older ice with fresh access to meteorites is exposed.

If you plan on following Lara's icy footsteps, prepare for an average temperature of -56°F/-49°C and severe wind chill. At nearly twice the size of Australia, Antarctica is a beautiful, hostile, and mostly desolate icescape. But those that make the journey will have the opportunity to view breathtaking sights, including glaciers, volcanos, and entire islands filled with penguins.

Lara crash-landed on Antarctica via helicopter. This is obviously not the recommended approach, though the real-world methods are not without risk. The most common route for tourist expeditions is through the Drake Passage, named after the famed explorer Sir Francis Drake. Powerful currents converge from three different oceans at the Drake Passage, resulting in waves reaching over sixty feet in height. During the early age of exploration, these conditions made the passage one of the most deadly sea voyages in the world. Luckily, modern maritime technology has reduced the most dangerous part of the voyage to severe seasickness.

Cruises usually depart from Ushuaia, Argentina, and after nearly fifty hours at sea you'll get access to the Antarctic coastline. The most popular destinations include King George Island, the Lemaire Channel, Deception Island, Port Lockroy, and Paradise Bay. Once on the coastline, you can catch activities including viewing icebergs from a zodiac boat, exploring via kayak, seal and penguin watching, and even camping on the coast.

The less common travel method is flying to Antarctica, with flights usually departing from Punta Arenas, Chile. Itineraries can be challenging considering the limited number of flights. Chartered flights are usually only available via tourism packages and are frequently delayed due to the destination's harsh weather. The flying season is also slim—usually December through February. However, flying allows you to enter mainland Antarctica, including the South Pole—albeit at a hefty price.

Sadly, you won't leave Antarctica with an official stamp on your passport due to the unique governance of the continent. However, there are souvenir stamps that can be obtained from research stations to chronicle your travels.

Thank you to our South American travel guide and recipe consultants: Freddy T. of Lara Croft Peru; Jorge Fernando Salazar Perdriel

SOUTH AMERICAN CUISINE
CANCHA SALADA

| ◐ **LOCATION:** SOUTH AMERICA | 🍶 **YIELD:** 2 CUPS | 🔥 **DIFFICULTY RATING:** 1 OUT OF 3 |

Roasted dried corn is a centuries-old crunchy Peruvian snack commonly served in bars or as an accompaniment to ceviche. The salty treat is a bit like corn nuts, or popcorn cooked inside of its shell, and uses extra-large kernels called maíz chulpe or cancha, which can often be found in Latin-American grocery stores.

☕ **PREP TIME:** 2 MINUTES   🍳 **COOK TIME:** 11 MINUTES

TOOLS NEEDED: Large pan with lid

INGREDIENTS:

2 tablespoons vegetable oil

2 cups cancha or maíz chulpe (dried)

1 tablespoon kosher salt

DIRECTIONS:

1. Prepare a large plate by lining it with paper towels. Heat the oil in a large pan over high heat.

2. Add the corn and cover the pan.

3. Shake the pan consistently to keep the corn moving while cooking. You may hear them pop and crack.

4. After about 10 minutes, or when the corn appears evenly golden brown and cracked and the popping sounds have stopped, pour the corn onto the prepared plate. Sprinkle with salt, let cool for a couple of minutes, then serve.

PICARONES

| **LOCATION:** VILCABAMBA, PERU | **YIELD:** 30 PICARONES | **DIFFICULTY RATING:** 3 OUT OF 3 |

Picarones are a type of doughnut made primarily from sweet potato and squash or pumpkin, then covered in syrup made from chancaca, or solidified molasses. The crispy exterior contrasts with the soft, flavorful interior. Picarones are traditionally served alongside anticuchos, a popular Peruvian meat skewer, resulting in a great sweet and salty combination.

RECIPE ORIGINS

Picarones were developed during the sixteenth-century colonial viceroyalty as an inexpensive replacement for the similar buñuelos, a fried fritter commonly served with a variety of fillings and toppings. The new, simpler dish rose in popularity and became a mainstay of modern Peruvian cuisine.

PREP TIME: 5 MINUTES | **COOK TIME:** 50 MINUTES | **INACTIVE TIME:** 2 HOURS AND 15 MINUTES

TOOLS NEEDED: Stand mixer with a dough hook, Kitchen towel, Deep pot or Dutch oven, for frying, Wooden spoon, Baking sheet

INGREDIENTS:

PICARONES:

1 pound sweet potatoes

2 star anise

¾ cup canned pumpkin puree

1 tablespoon active dry yeast

1 tablespoon granulated sugar

⅛ teaspoon kosher salt

4 cups all-purpose flour

4 cups vegetable oil

SYRUP:

2 pieces of chancaca or ¼ cup molasses

1½ cups light brown sugar, packed

½ cup water

2 cinnamon sticks

6 cloves

2 star anise

1 orange

2 limes

DIRECTIONS:

1. Peel the sweet potatoes and cut them into 1-inch chunks. Place the potatoes and star anise in a large pot of water, and boil for 12 to 15 minutes, or until the potatoes can be pierced easily with a fork.

2. Drain, reserving one cup of water, remove the star anise, and mash the potatoes until they're smooth. Let cool for 5 minutes, and mix in the pumpkin puree.

3. Once the reserve water has cooled to a lukewarm temperature, place the water, yeast, and sugar in a large mixing bowl. Let stand for 10 minutes or until foamy.

4. Add the pumpkin puree and sweet potato mixture, and mix on low with a dough hook attachment until fully combined.

5. Add the salt and the flour in ½ cup increments, and mix until the dough is smooth. If the dough is too sticky, add additional flour ½ cup at a time.

6. Cover the bowl with a damp towel and let rise for 2 hours, or until the dough has doubled in size.

Continued on page 32

Continued from page 31

7. While the dough is rising, make the syrup. If using chancaca, cut it into small pieces and put in a pot (or put the molasses straight in the pot) with the brown sugar, water, cinnamon sticks, cloves, and star anise. Cut the orange and limes in half, squeeze the juice out into the pot, and place the rind in as well. Mix the contents of the pot together. Bring to a boil, then lower the heat and simmer for 15 minutes or until the sugars have all dissolved and the syrup has thickened slightly. Strain, and store the syrup in a jar. Place the jar in the refrigerator to cool.

8. Pour the oil into a large heavy pot or Dutch oven and heat to 350°F. Place a bowl of cold water off to the side.

9. Dip your hands in the cold water and then rip off a small chunk of dough, a little smaller than the palm of your hand. Use your thumb to poke a hole through the middle and slightly stretch the dough into a ring as you gently put it in the hot oil. Place the handle of a wooden spoon in the hole and rotate it around, spinning the dough to help guide it into a rounder shape. After one side has puffed up and become golden brown (about 2 minutes), use the spoon handle to flip it over to the other side. Cook for 2 additional minutes, until both sides are evenly browned.

10. Place the finished picarones on a paper towel-covered baking sheet to drain.

11. Plate the picarones, cover with syrup, and eat while still warm.

LOCATION FEATURED IN:
Tomb Raider (1996),
Tomb Raider: Anniversary (2007)

KEY LOCATION:
City of Vilcabamba

MEMORABLE MOMENT:
Taking your first steps as Lara Croft

LOMO SALTADO

Lomo saltado is a traditional Peruvian stir-fry combining marinated beef, tomatoes, and vegetables. "Lomo saltado" means "jumping loin" and represents the act of stir-frying the tenderloin used in the dish. It is commonly served with rice and French fries, an indicator of its hybrid origins. The wide array of potential ingredients and the presentation of the fries allows for great personalization of the hearty recipe. If you can't find an aji amarillo, substitute a yellow bell pepper and jalapeño pepper.

RECIPE ORIGINS

Lomo saltado originates from Chifa, a culinary fusion invented by Chinese immigrants who settled in Peru around the turn of the twentieth century. Chifa fuses Cantonese cuisine with Peruvian ingredients and influences. Chifa creations such as lomo saltado have since become some of Peru's most beloved dishes.

⏱ PREP TIME: 70 MINUTES   **⏱ COOK TIME:** 50 MINUTES

TOOLS NEEDED: Deep pot or Dutch oven, for frying, Kitchen thermometer, Large wok or frying pan, Blender

INGREDIENTS:

1 pound (about 3) russet potatoes

Vegetable oil, for frying

Salt and black pepper, to taste

3 tablespoons soy sauce

1½ tablespoons white vinegar

3 cloves garlic, minced

2 teaspoons cumin

1 pound tenderloin steak

½ red onion, cut into thin wedges

2 plum tomatoes, cut into wedges

1 yellow chili pepper (aji amarillo, if available), stemmed, seeded, and sliced lengthwise

1 tablespoon minced cilantro

White rice, cooked

DIRECTIONS:

1. To make the fries: Peel the potatoes and cut them into ½-inch strips. Soak the potato strips in cold water for at least 1 hour, then rinse and pat dry.

2. Heat 3 inches of vegetable oil in a large, heavy pot to 325°F. Using a slotted spoon, place some of the fries in (enough where they are fully submerged and not overcrowded). Cook the fries for 5 to 6 minutes, then remove and set them on a paper towel–lined plate. Continue with all the fries.

3. Heat the oil up to 400°F, and cook each batch of fries a second time until they are crisp and golden brown (about 5 minutes). This will help make an extra crispy fry. Set on a paper towel–lined plate, salt to taste, and set aside.

4. For the stir-fry sauce: In a small bowl, mix together the soy sauce, vinegar, garlic, and cumin. Set aside.

5. For the stir-fry: Slicing against the grain, cut the steak into thin strips (about ¼-inch thick). Salt and pepper the steak.

6. Heat 2 tablespoons of oil in a large frying pan or wok over high heat. Add the steak, and cook for 1 minute on each side or until browned. Make sure the steak has room in the pan to sear—if it's touching other pieces, fry in multiple batches.

7. Remove from the pan, and set aside.

8. Add the onion to the pan, and cook for 3 minutes, or until the onions are browned and softened.

Continued on page 36

Continued from page 35

9. Add the tomato and pepper to the onions, and cook for another 3 minutes. You want the pepper and tomato to be only slightly softened.

10. Add the stir-fry sauce to the large pan, and stir to combine. Cook for an additional 1 minute.

11. Add the steak, all its juices, and the cilantro, and mix together. Mix in the fries at the last possible moment, so they don't get soggy.

12. Serve with a scoop of white rice. If you want to add a bit of heat, top your lomo saltado with some aji verde.

AJI VERDE

INGREDIENTS:

½ cup mayonnaise

2 tablespoons lime juice

1 large bunch of cilantro (about 2 cups), coarsely chopped

1 clove garlic, coarsely chopped

1 tablespoon aji amarillo paste (or 1 tablespoon seeded and coarsely chopped jalapeño)

2 teaspoons huacatay paste (or 1 tablespoon chopped fresh mint)

2 tablespoons cotija cheese (or 2 tablespoons grated parmesan)

¼ teaspoon kosher salt

¼ teaspoon black pepper

DIRECTIONS:

13. In a blender, blend the mayonnaise, lime juice, cilantro, garlic, aji amarillo paste, huacatay paste, cotija, salt, and pepper until smooth. Chill for at least 1 hour before serving.

LOCATION FEATURED IN:
Shadow of the Tomb Raider (2018)

KEY LOCATION:
Crash site

MEMORABLE MOMENT:
Fighting the Empress Jaguar

PERUVIAN CUISINE
CEVICHE

| **LOCATION:** PARAISO, PERU | **YIELD:** 6 SERVINGS | **DIFFICULTY RATING:** 1 OUT OF 3 |

While not as adventurous as consuming poisonous pufferfish, ceviche can be dangerous when not prepared with precision. The meal requires fresh raw fish to be marinated in a citrus-vinegar mixture and seasoned with spices, then served immediately. Citric acid from the lemon and lime commonly used to prepare ceviche gives the appearance of the fish being cooked after only a matter of minutes. However, acidic marinades do not eliminate bacteria or parasites, presenting a serious health hazard when prepared incorrectly.

RECIPE ORIGINS

This Peruvian national dish is said to originate from the Moche, a civilization from the northern coast of Peru dating back roughly two millennia ago. Ceviche or similar dishes are common throughout the Americas. Ecuadorian ceviche, for example, is prepared with shrimp and tomato sauce, while Mexican variants are often prepared in a cocktail dish and paired with tostadas.

PREP TIME: 10 MINUTES   **COOK TIME:** 30 MINUTES

TOOLS NEEDED: Large glass bowl, Steamer (or steamer basket for a pot)

INGREDIENTS:

1½ pounds of a fresh, firm white fish (sea bass, corvina, halibut, or mahi mahi)

½ red onion, halved and sliced thin

1 cup key lime juice (or regular limes, if key limes/Peruvian limes are not available)

1½ teaspoons kosher salt

1 habanero pepper, seeded, halved, and thinly sliced

2 tablespoons aji amarillo paste (or an additional habanero pepper)

1 small sweet potato, peeled and cut into thick rounds

1 ear of corn, husked

½ cup chopped cilantro

6 butter lettuce leaves

DIRECTIONS:

1. Cut the fish into ¾-inch cubes (removing any skin or bones in the process), and rinse in cold water with the red onion. Drain the water.

2. Combine the fish, onion, lime juice, salt, pepper, and aji amarillo paste in a large glass bowl, making sure that the lime juice covers as much of the fish as possible. Cover with plastic wrap and refrigerate for 30 minutes, mixing once halfway through. The acid from the lime juice will "cook" the fish. You'll know it's done when the fish appears opaque and white.

3. While the fish is "cooking," steam the sweet potato for 7 minutes and the ear of corn for 3 minutes, until soft. Cut the corn off of the cob.

4. Place a scoop of the ceviche on each plate. Top with chopped cilantro leaves, and plate alongside a sweet potato slice, some steamed corn, and a butter lettuce leaf.

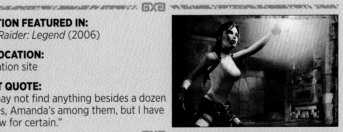

LOCATION FEATURED IN:
Tomb Raider: Legend (2006)

KEY LOCATION:
Excavation site

CROFT QUOTE:
"We may not find anything besides a dozen corpses, Amanda's among them, but I have to know for certain."

BOLIVIAN CUISINE
SALTEÑAS

| ⊙ **LOCATION:** TIWANAKU, BOLIVIA | 🗍 **YIELD:** 15 SALTEÑAS | ⚡ **DIFFICULTY RATING:** 3 OUT OF 3 |

Salteñas are a sweet and savory empanada made of meat or vegetables. The filling traditionally contains potatoes and sometimes olives and raisins with a hint of spice. The filling, known as "jigote," is prepared as a gelatinous stew and refrigerated before being baked, resulting in flavorful juiciness without causing the pastry to become soggy during the process. Salteñas are an essential gift for Father's Day, whereas Mother's Day often features far more elaborate meals and gifts, though this is mostly a joke among Bolivians.

RECIPE ORIGINS

Historians claim the recipe was invented by Juana Manuela Gorriti, an Argentinian exile who moved to Bolivia and later married the country's eleventh president, Manuel Isidoro Belzu. Gorriti's family was extremely impoverished, and creating salteñas allowed them to make a living. The dish's name was inspired by Gorriti's hometown of Salta, Argentina.

🕐 **PREP TIME:** 10 MINUTES   🕐 **COOK TIME:** 70 MINUTES   🕐 **INACTIVE TIME:** 4 HOURS

TOOLS NEEDED: Pot, Large skillet or Dutch oven, Small saucepan, Casserole dish, Rolling pin, Parchment paper, Baking sheet

INGREDIENTS:

FILLING:

1 tablespoon vegetable oil

½ pound stewing beef, diced in ½-inch cubes

½ red bell pepper, seeded and diced

½ yellow onion, diced

½ tablespoon aji panca powder or paste (or ¼ tablespoon cayenne pepper)

½ teaspoon cumin

½ teaspoon smoked paprika

½ teaspoon oregano

Salt and black pepper, to taste

2 cups beef broth

1 large russet potato, peeled and diced into ½-inch cubes

¼ cup frozen peas

1 (¼-ounce) package unflavored gelatin

½ cup cold water

¼ cup green olives, sliced (or black olives, sliced)

1 hard-boiled egg, sliced

FILLING DIRECTIONS:

1. Heat the vegetable oil in a large, heavy skillet or Dutch oven on medium-high, and add the beef cubes. Sauté, stirring often, until browned on all sides but not fully cooked through, about 2 to 3 minutes. Remove the beef and set aside.

2. Add the bell pepper, onion, and aji panca to the skillet, and sauté for 3 to 4 minutes or until the pepper and onion have softened.

3. Add the cumin, smoked paprika, and oregano, and then add salt and pepper to taste. Sauté for 2 more minutes or until fragrant.

4. Add the beef and beef broth, and bring to a boil. Turn the temperature to low, and simmer for 30 minutes.

5. Place the potato cubes in a pot of boiling water. Simmer for 5 minutes or until the potatoes can be pierced with a fork but are still firm enough to hold their shape. Drain and set the potatoes aside.

6. Add the potatoes and peas to the stew.

7. Dissolve the gelatin in the cold water. Once fully dissolved, add the gelatin mixture to the beef stew. Mix well.

8. Transfer the stew to a casserole dish, cover, and refrigerate for 4 hours, or until completely chilled.

Continued on page 40

Continued from page 39

DOUGH:

4 tablespoons (¼ cup) salted butter

¼ cup vegetable shortening

1 tablespoon achiote (or ½ tablespoon paprika and ½ tablespoon turmeric)

4 cups all-purpose flour

¼ cup granulated sugar

1 teaspoon kosher salt

1 egg

¾ cup hot water

2 egg whites, whisked, for brushing the tops of the salteñas

DOUGH DIRECTIONS:

9. Combine the butter, shortening, and achiote in a small saucepan, and heat over medium until everything is melted and mixed through. Remove from heat.

10. Mix together the flour, sugar, and salt in a large bowl, and then incorporate the butter mixture. Once everything is fully mixed, add the egg and mix until all traces of the egg are gone. Slowly mix in the hot water.

11. Knead for 2 minutes with a mixer or 4 minutes by hand until it forms a smooth dough.

12. Cover the bowl and set aside for 30 minutes.

SALTEÑA DIRECTIONS:

13. Preheat the oven to 450°F.

14. Divide the dough into 15 small balls. Press the balls into flat, round discs, and let rest for 5 minutes.

15. One at a time, roll each disc with a rolling pin until they're about 6 inches in diameter and ⅛-inch thick.

16. Place 2 tablespoons of filling in the middle of the disc, then top with a couple of olive slices and a hard-boiled egg slice.

17. Bring up both sides of the dough so they meet above the filling, pinch the edges together, and fold the tops over slightly, making a secure seam directly above the middle.

18. Brush the top with a little bit of a whisked egg white, and place on a parchment paper–covered baking sheet.

19. Repeat with the rest of the salteñas.

20. Bake for 15 to 20 minutes or until golden brown.

21. When eating, hold vertically and start on one of the ends, so the liquid filling doesn't fall out.

LOCATION FEATURED IN:
Tomb Raider: Legend (2006)

KEY LOCATION:
Ruins of Tiwanaku

MEMORABLE MOMENT:
Ascending

ANTARCTIC CUISINE
SLEDGING BISCUITS

◁❿ LOCATION: UNDISCLOSED, ANTARCTICA **┃ 🥫 YIELD:** 8 BISCUITS ┃ 🔥 **DIFFICULTY RATING:** 1 OUT OF 3

These high-calorie, high-energy survival snacks have been crucial in the harsh Antarctic for centuries. The lack of flavor is a small sacrifice compared to the compact, long-lasting, and life-saving nature of the biscuits. For those making sledging biscuits from the comfort (and warmth) of their own homes, the biscuits can be embellished upon considerably. Usually they are topped with large amounts of butter or cheese, or paired with Antarctic pemmican—foodstuff made from lean beef and fat. Combine the two to get Antarctic hoosh, a stew made from sledging biscuits, pemmican, and snow. Do be mindful of the calories, as genuine sledging biscuits and their accompanying dishes can easily skyrocket into the thousands per serving.

🕐 **PREP TIME:** 5 MINUTES   🕐 **COOK TIME:** 25 MINUTES

TOOLS NEEDED: Medium bowl, Rolling pin, Baking sheet, Wire rack

INGREDIENTS:

1 cup all-purpose flour

½ teaspoon salt

½ teaspoon baking powder

2 tablespoons unsalted butter, cold

3 tablespoons cold water

DIRECTIONS:

1. Preheat the oven to 375°F.

2. Mix together the flour, salt, and baking powder in a medium bowl. Cut the butter into the mixture, using your fingers to rub it together. Continue until the mixture starts to resemble crumbs.

3. Slowly mix in the cold water until a dough forms.

4. Place the dough on a floured surface and roll it out into a rectangle about ½-inch thick. Cut the rectangle into 8 smaller rectangles, approximately 2 inches long.

5. Place the bars on a parchment paper–covered baking sheet, and prick each bar with a fork to create tiny holes throughout the top.

6. Bake for 15 minutes. The biscuits won't brown up much, but they'll be done.

7. Transfer to a wire rack to cool.

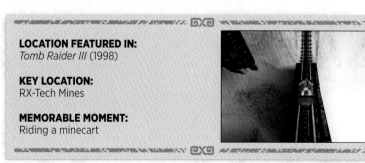

LOCATION FEATURED IN:
Tomb Raider III (1998)

KEY LOCATION:
RX-Tech Mines

MEMORABLE MOMENT:
Riding a minecart

ANTARCTIC CUISINE
TOMATO SOUP

Tomatoes have long had an identity crisis. Not only is the fruit commonly mistaken for a vegetable, but tomatoes were also once believed to be extremely poisonous, earning them the name "wolfpeach" by renowned the French botanist Joseph Pitton de Tournefort. He was half-correct. While tomatoes are safe to consume (and highly nutritious), their leaves are toxic in large quantities.

Tomato soup has no such identity crisis. No matter how it's made—creamy, condensed, dried, hot or cold, with meatballs and vegetables—the flexible soup is famous around the world for its simplicity, versatility, and comfort. If you're considering a trip to Antarctica, however, the warmer variety and a quality thermos are highly recommended. Tomb Raider III (1998) antagonist Dr. Willard can be seen enjoying a hot bowl of tomato soup when confronted by Lara, so this particular recipe uses shelf-stable ingredients that could survive transport to Antarctica.

RECIPE ORIGINS

The first known published recipe for tomato soup was in the *New Cookery Book* by Eliza Leslie in 1857. Forty years later, American entrepreneur Joseph A. Campbell's recipe for condensed tomato soup helped his company, Campbell Soup Company, become synonymous with canned soup.

🕐 **PREP TIME:** 5 MINUTES   🕐 **COOK TIME:** 40 MINUTES

TOOLS NEEDED: Soup pot, Immersion blender or standard blender

INGREDIENTS:

2 tablespoons olive oil

1 yellow onion, diced

3 cloves garlic, minced

1 (28-ounce) can of whole peeled tomatoes and its juice

1 (6-ounce) can of tomato paste

3 cups vegetable broth

1 tablespoon granulated sugar

2 teaspoons dried basil

1 teaspoon kosher salt

¼ teaspoon black pepper

Additional salt and pepper, to taste

DIRECTIONS:

1. Heat the olive oil in a large soup pot over medium-high heat, and add the onion and garlic. Cook for 5 minutes, or until onion is softened and translucent.

2. Add the tomatoes, tomato paste, vegetable broth, sugar, basil, salt, and pepper. Bring to a boil, then reduce the heat to low.

3. Simmer for 30 minutes. Salt and pepper to taste, and then remove the pot from the heat.

4. Using an immersion blender, puree the soup until smooth. If you don't have an immersion blender, carefully pour the soup into a blender in batches.

5. Divide between four soup bowls and serve hot.

LOCATION FEATURED IN:
Tomb Raider III (1998)

KEY LOCATION:
RX Technologies research base

UNIQUE VEHICLE:
Inflatable Boat

CHAPTER THREE
EUROPE

◑ **KEY LOCATIONS:** Surrey, London, Dover, and Cornwall, England; Scottish Highlands, Scotland; Undisclosed, Greece; Venice and Rome, Italy; Black Isle, Ireland; Paris, France; Prague, Czech Republic; Arctic Circle, Norway; Mediterranean Sea

Key Terminology:

- **Western Civilization/World:** A Eurocentric catchall term for modern cultures throughout Europe, the Americas, and colonized areas with shared European heritage including political systems, belief systems, and values with a strong foundational influence from Greco-Roman civilization. This is not a geographic term, as Australia is generally considered part of the western civilization/world.

- **Continental Europe:** A geographic term that refers to mainland Europe.

- **England:** An island country northwest of the European continent.

- **Great Britain:** The term for the rest of the island when you add the bordering countries of Scotland to the North and Wales to the West.

- **United Kingdom:** When you factor in Northern Ireland, the group becomes the United Kingdom of Great Britain and Northern Ireland.

- **Scandinavia:** A geographical subregion of Europe. The definition varies from country to country, used in the strictest way to describe Sweden, Norway, and Denmark, or generalized to also include northern countries of Finland, Iceland, Greenland, the Faroe Islands, and other small island chains.

- **Mediterranean Basin:** A term used to describe areas of land around the Mediterranean Sea across Europe, Asia, and Africa that have similar climate and vegetation.

- **Eurasia:** A term describing the continental area of Europe and Asia, used to refer to the geographic land mass as opposed to the socially constructed division between the two.

- **Arctic Circle:** The most northerly circle of latitude on maps of Earth, and home to the arctic region.

Europe's borders are defined by its natural features—the Arctic Ocean to the north, the Ural Mountains to the east, the Mediterranean and neighboring seas to the south, and the Atlantic Ocean to the west. Impressive mountain ranges flatten out into the Great European Plain as you move east across Europe, and the fjords of the Scandinavian peninsula are contrasted by the warm Mediterranean coastlines as you move toward the equator.

Considered the cradle of Western civilization, much of modern society in the West was established in Europe. This includes shared values, traditions, political systems, religions, arts, and technology. Ancient Greece is credited as the birthplace of democracy, and the Roman Empire refined government and law's place in society. Movements like the Renaissance and the scientific revolution played key roles in the evolution of Western humanities and science. The rise of Christianity also held much sway over the Europe of today, which in turn became true of many other parts of the world. European religions, values, art, and customs spread and often replaced the heritages of indigenous cultures through colonialism.

Existing entirely in the Northern Hemisphere, the Europe of today packs an impressive number of countries and cultures into a relatively small space, ranging in size from the sovereign city-state of Vatican City to the westernmost part of Russia—the largest country in the world. This diversity offers nearly limitless ancient sites and modern marvels to explore across Europe.

Although hundreds of indigenous languages have been documented throughout Europe, today most countries speak branches of three primary languages, which reflect the continent's storied past. Popular Romance languages—from the Roman Empire's Latin—include French, Italian, Spanish, and Portuguese. English, German, Dutch, Swedish, Norwegian, and more fall into Germanic languages and were born of Scandinavia's early Iron Age. Slavic languages become more common as you move east across Europe, and encompass Russian, Ukrainian, and Polish, among others, and had a start in the Early Middle Ages. Other popular languages include those with Celtic, Baltic, and Greek origins.

With over five hundred national parks across the varied terrain of Europe, there is much to explore outside of metropolitan areas. You can get breathtaking views of the French Alps in Écrins National Park and hike among the Pyrenees in Spain's Ordesa National Park. If you venture north to Iceland's Vatnajökull National Park, natural ice caves and glaciers are open for exploration. The untouched Wild Taiga of Finland is exquisite for wildlife viewing, and there is nothing quite like Plitvice Lakes National Park in Croatia, which is home to an almost surreal network of terraced lakes and waterfalls.

One of the marvels of modern Europe is its interconnectedness—short flights between countries and comfy train rides can take you from one end of the continent to the other. Additionally, residents of the European Union benefit from passport-free zones in most EU countries, which streamlines the travel.

Lara didn't have to stray far from her native England to find adventure. Her many European exploits include boating through the Venice canals in *Tomb Raider II* (1997) as well as fighting lions in the Roman Colosseum and exploring the haunted isles of Ireland as a teenager in *Tomb Raider: Chronicles* (2000).

SURREY, ENGLAND

Surrey, a county in southeast England, is home to the fictional Croft Manor. In the Tomb Raider universe, Croft Manor is a perfect place for Lara to prepare for her adventures—complete with a library, gymnasium, hidden trophy room, obstacle/assault course, ATV track, and hedge maze, along with the more common accommodations. Croft Manor holds a special place in fans' hearts since the series debut, and many Tomb Raider fans who travel to England seek out a Croft-like estate to visit.

According to the original Croft Manor level designer, Heather Gibson, the architecture isn't tied to a specific structure, but rather was inspired by common countryside aesthetics. That being said, fans have noticed some similarities between Croft Manor and Compton Wynyates, a Tudor-period home located in Warwickshire, England. The estate is a private home, so it isn't open for visitation. There is an alternative stop in Surrey, found in King Henry VIII's Hampton Court Palace. A stunning Tudor complex with equally beautiful grounds, fans will enjoy the garden maze in particular.

Moving out of Surrey, Hatfield House in Hertfordshire has served as the new facade for Croft Manor starting with the first film starring Angelina Jolie—*Tomb Raider* (2001). A beautiful Jacobean structure, Hatfield House was completed in 1611. It is one of the ten palaces, houses, and castles that make up the Treasure Houses of England, a consortium of estates geared toward tourism.

Tours of the house are a must, with highlights including the Marble Hall, Grand Staircase, King James Drawing Room, the Long Gallery, and the Armory. There is also a massive library with over ten thousand books ranging from the sixteenth century onward. Each room houses art and artifacts that are treasures in their own right, such as the Rainbow Portrait of Queen Elizabeth I.

The nearby Old Palace, built in 1485, showcases beautiful medieval brickwork, and the garden walks are equally stunning; the famous East Garden in particular is full of meticulously groomed topiaries.

Hatfield House welcomes visitors on a seasonal basis, so be sure to check the calendar before you plan your trip. Located twenty miles north of Central London, it's an easy commute by bus or train, disembarking at the Hatfield Railway Station.

LONDON, ENGLAND

The capital of England and the largest city in the United Kingdom, London is a massive metropolitan area full of popular tourist spots. In *Tomb Raider III* (1998), Lara manages to find a few unusual locations while searching for an artifact known as the Eye of Isis.

Lara starts her London adventure in Thames Wharf, but doesn't spend much time at ground level. She's mostly seen zipping around the city rooftops with the beautiful dome of St. Paul's Cathedral in the background. If you're looking for a unique perspective of London, a safer alternative is one of the many Thames river cruises.

If it's a higher vantage point you're after, St. Paul's Cathedral offers a breathtaking view of London for those willing to put in the work. The cathedral is open all week except Sundays, and buying a ticket grants you entry to not only the church but also to the galleries of historical objects, tombs, and the domes high above. Make sure to stretch properly before climbing the 259 steps to the interior dome

and the Whispering Gallery, where the acoustics are impeccable. Climbing a total of 528 steps will get you access to the Golden Gallery and a view of the city that doesn't require rooftop access.

Next on Lara's itinerary is Aldwych Station, previously known as Strand Station when it opened in 1907. Located in Central London, Aldwych closed in 1994 due to dwindling usage, but has a seasoned history outside of transportation. It was used as a shelter for both people and art during World War I and II, and is now used for filming movies such as *V for Vendetta* and *Sherlock*. Tours of the station are available, but they sell out quickly, so it's best to sign up for the waiting list via the London Transport Museum website. For those of you at home, you can also sign up for a virtual tour, which includes extra access and a Q&A at the end.

In the Lud's Gate level, Lara is off to visit the Natural History Museum to steal some embalming fluid for new friends she met in the abandoned train station. She proceeds to shimmy through ducts and open trap doors to gain access to an Egyptian exhibit. While the Natural History Museum is explicitly mentioned in-game, the exhibit is actually inspired by the world-renowned British Museum, which has over fifty thousand Egyptian objects in its collection. Despite the creative liberty, we still highly recommend a stop at the Natural History Museum to say hello to an old friend; the famous Dinosaur Gallery is home to the first T. rex skeleton ever discovered. Both museums merit a full day dedicated to exploring their labyrinthine galleries, but you can also take shorter tours to get the highlights if you're on a tight itinerary. Better yet, they are both free to visit, so they are perfect for budget-conscious travelers.

CORNWALL, ENGLAND

Continuing her home-base adventures, Lara also explores the county of Cornwall in *Tomb Raider: Legend* (2006), located in the most southwest part of England. She is in search of a piece of the legendary sword Excalibur and finds it in King Arthur's tomb, hidden below a kitschy Arthurian museum.

Cornwall is a location where many legends of King Arthur were born, so it isn't surprising there are a number of dedicated tours available for travelers. The must-see stops include the castle near the village of Tintagel, where Arthur is rumored to have been conceived. This and many other local legends are subject to debate, as is the legitimacy of Arthur himself as a real historical figure. What isn't up for debate is the beauty of Tintagel Castle's ruins against

the stunning seascape. The stronghold was built in the thirteenth century, half on the mainland and half on a cliff jutting into the Cornish Sea. It was only in 2019 that a bridge once again united the two sections, which had been divided for five hundred years.

Cornwall also boasts other sites tied to Arthurian lore, including St. Nectan's Glen, where his knights were supposedly blessed as they departed in search of the Holy Grail. The aptly named Slaughterbridge is found nearby, rumored to be the place of Arthur's final battle. The nearby town of Camelford has been tied to Camelot of legend, although that too is disputed. While the truth may be lost to time, Cornwall is an excellent place to brush up on your history of one of the most legendary figures of all time.

DOVER, ENGLAND

Lara's *Tomb Raider III* (1998) adventure is extended in an expansion pack called *The Lost Artifact* (2000), in which she searches for a fifth meteorite only recently brought to her attention. One of her stops is Dover in the county of Kent, known as the Garden of England and home to the famous White Cliffs of Dover. The level—Shakespeare Cliff—doesn't show off much of the stunning seascape, so we'd suggest you not muck about in active drill sites and instead skip right to the good stuff.

The white cliffs face the Strait of Dover and are close enough to France that you can see land on a clear day. The proximity is why the nearby town of Folkestone was chosen as the point of departure for the undersea Channel Tunnel—called the Chunnel for short—which connects England to Northern France by train. Hence the drilling escapades in Lara's adventure.

Only a two-to-three-hour train ride southeast from London, the Cliffs of Dover extend on both sides of the city, reaching a height of 350 feet. They are renowned for their striking white appearance due to the high amount of chalk in their composition. Shakespeare's Cliff is on the south side of Dover and is said to be named for the inspiration it served him when writing *King Lear*.

While the cliffs are certainly a must-see, be sure not to skip over the city of Dover itself. There are designated walking routes that will guide you through the major sights, starting with the huge medieval Dover Castle, along the cliffs, and to the nearby Deal Castle.

SCOTTISH HIGHLANDS

In *Tomb Raider III: The Lost Artifact* (2000), the meteorite-driven mystery also includes a visit to the departed Dr. Willard's Loch Ness estate in the Scottish Highlands. Most people know Loch Ness—a freshwater lake that feeds into the River Ness, and eventually to the North Sea—by the alleged monster that haunts it. While spotting Nessy is unlikely, the loch boasts lots to see in the surrounding area.

If you're looking for ruins to explore, Drumnadrochit's Urquhart Castle overlooking Loch Ness is quite similar to those in *Tomb Raider III: The Lost Artifact* (2000). One of Scotland's largest castles, the site was once home to a medieval fortress and played a role in the Wars of Scottish Independence. Later, it became a royal castle until being partially destroyed in the late sixteenth century.

The Scottish Highlands themselves are a sight to behold, showcased particularly well in the nearby Cairngorms National Park. The largest national park in the United Kingdom, Cairngorms is home to four of the five tallest mountains in Scotland and is ripe with opportunities to enjoy the outdoors via hiking, biking, skiing, and camping. You can also search for the free-grazing Cairngorm reindeer, check out a slew of other castles, or visit iconic whisky distilleries. It's suggested you spend at least one day in the Cairngorms National Park, but you could easily spend a week in the wilderness and have much left to explore.

UNDISCLOSED, GREECE

Lara's trip to Greece in the original *Tomb Raider* (1996) is uniquely memorable for offering an array of experiences in a single locale: the dizzying heights of St. Francis's Folly, the deadly encounters of the Colosseum, a legendary death in Palace Midas, and an endless maze of water in the Cistern.

Perched atop a massive cliff, the monastery dedicated to St. Francis has striking similarities with the Meteora Eastern Orthodox monasteries located in the Thessaly area of Greece. Meteora means "lofty," "suspended," or "elevated" which is exactly what these structures are, sitting over one thousand feet off the ground. Reachable by train from Athens, there are six monasteries remaining of the original twenty, built up on massive rock pillars between the fourteenth and sixteenth centuries. At the time they provided great protection from the changing political tides, as the only way up was a rope ladder or net, which could be quickly retracted if needed.

All six monasteries are still used today; two house nuns and the other four are home to monks. Since they are active places of worship, be mindful to dress appropriately on your visit. If you don't have the time to see them all, Great Meteoron—the largest of the six and the main museum for tourists—Varlaam, and St. Stephen's offer a good swath of the experience. Fortunately there are now steps to each monastery— ranging from 150 to 300—so no rope ladders are necessary. Steady shoes are, though.

As for the Colosseum, amphitheaters are common throughout Greece, built into hillsides and featuring tiered seating. Roman amphitheaters are similar in style, but also include freestanding structures. In Athens you can see both the Roman theater Odeon of Herodes Atticus and the much older ancient Greek theater of Dionysus. Both are located in the Acropolis of Athens—home to the renowned Parthenon—making it easy to access all three in one day.

A trip to the neighboring country of Turkey is in order to see a Cistern of Tomb Raider scale. The Basilica Cistern in Istanbul is supported by over three hundred marble columns. It holds little water now, trading utility to become a unique tourist destination. Since King Midas also ruled over the area known as Phrygia in the west-central part of Anatolia, Tomb Raider's tie to Turkey is twofold.

Tomb Raider's (1996) larger narrative is also framed within Greek mythology. That being said, the lost island of Atlantis Lara discovers isn't quite what one would expect. Instead of ancient ruins, Lara uncovers advanced technology harnessed by Natla to create a mutant Atlantean army.

The Greek islands of Santorini are often linked to the origin story of Atlantis. The downfall of the Minoan civilization—the Minoans of Crete—due to a catastrophic volcanic eruption adds more credence to the theory that islands of the Aegean Sea were home to Atlantis. You can even see a reference to the dolphin fresco from Knossos—the most famous of Crete's Minoan palaces— in a pool Lara swims through at St. Francis's Folly.

VENICE, ITALY

One of Europe's most famous tourist locations, the floating city of Venice in northeast Italy is on many bucket lists. Venice isn't a single island, but rather a series of over one hundred islands in a shallow lagoon, connected with several hundred bridges and often traversed by boat. Lara eagerly takes advantage of the water-based transport in *Tomb Raider II* (1997), as she drives the franchise's first-ever vehicle through the canals—a speedboat.

When you visit Venice, you will likely be traveling at a lower speed via large water buses called vaporetti, or the iconic gondolas—although the former is notably less expensive. Both let you take in the scenery from Venice's canals, especially the Grand Canal and the famous Rialto Bridge.

When exploring the city itself, you'll be traveling by foot, so pack light and wear comfortable shoes. Be sure to check out the St. Mark's Basilica at the eastern end of St. Mark's Square. The basilica is the most famous in the city and is a stunning blend of Italian and Byzantine architecture.

If you're in the mood for opera—from the audience's perspective, rather than Lara's unauthorized backstage access—Teatro La Fenice is recommended. An essential site in the history of opera and home to the premieres of major composers, the theater name translates to "Theater of the Phoenix." It's an apt name, as the structure has endured three big fires since opening in 1792. Still, it is one of Italy's most stunning opera houses.

Spring and fall are considered the best time to visit Venice, to avoid the sweltering humidity or freezing conditions, and many businesses close down in the off-season. If you are able, it's best to stay on the historic central main island—Centro Storico—rather than commuting over the two-mile Ponte della Libertà bridge each day. This also allows you to wander the streets of Venice in the early hours and late at night, after cruise ships have departed and the overwhelming crowds with them.

ROME, ITALY

Lara's second Italian adventure is told through the eyes of her associates in *Tomb Raider: Chronicles* (2000), kicking off in the streets of Rome. While the exact location is not noted, the neighborhood of Monti is a great one to explore on foot. From it you can walk to historic sites like the Trevi Fountain, Pantheon, Roman Forum, Temple of Saturn, Basilica of Saint Mary Major, and several museums with a focus on the city's history. You can't walk a block without running into a point of interest from antiquity—in fact, it may surprise you how often ancient and modern structures intertwine in Rome.

You can also walk to the nearby Trajan's Market, a specific spot Lara explores. A series of ruins located near the Colosseum, these markets would have been the equivalent of an ancient shopping mall. A covered complex of sturdy brick and concrete, they were strong enough to stack shops, apartments, and offices six stories high. Built for the emperor Trajan around 110 CE, the market is located across from his namesake forum, which is also very much worth a visit. Both Trajan's Forum and Trajan's Market were designed

by his favorite architect, Apollodorus of Damascus, whose design eye and engineering insights ensured his name was not lost to the ages.

Lara saves the most magnificent stop for last, exploring the iconic Colosseum, now designated one of the New Seven Wonders of the World. A popular theory is that the freestanding Roman amphitheater got its name for the large bronze statue—also known as a colossus—of Emperor Nero that flanked the structure for a time.

Built over the course of a decade, starting in 70 CE, the Colosseum was an active cultural site for over five hundred years and could hold upwards of fifty thousand people. A gift to Rome's people, the Colosseum was a center point of society, home to mythological dramas, battle reenactments, animal hunts, public executions, and, most famously, gladiatorial events. Over the centuries the Colosseum fell into disrepair due to earthquakes, looting for new construction, and the ravages of time, although it continues to be one of the largest tourist attractions in the world.

BLACK ISLE, IRELAND

Young Lara Croft's adventure in *Tomb Raider: Chronicles* (2000) begins after she stows away on a boat headed for Ireland's fictional Black Isle. Armed only with her wits, Lara unknowingly becomes involved with a troublesome case of demonic possession, encountering ghosts, ghouls, and Fae along the way. Several of these creatures resemble those from Irish folklore, including small-statured imps akin to classical Irish changelings or the goblin-like pooka. She also survives a close encounter with a ghastly underwater creature inspired by the Merrow, and is guided safely through a labyrinth by lights strikingly similar to will-o'-the-wisp. Fae of lore are diverse in nature; some good, some bad, and many fond of playing tricks.

Ireland is a country that eagerly embraces both modernity and mythology, and spooky stories certainly have a place in Irish lore. Some academics believe Ireland is even the birthplace of the celebration that inspired Halloween, before it was Christianized into the more familiar All Hallows' Eve. The traditional Celtic festival of Samhain (Irish for "summer's end") was a celebration of the changing seasons and the start of the darker half of the year. Beginning on October 31, it was believed that the veil between worlds was the thinnest and that ghosts of loved ones and Fae could enter the land of the living. This also meant that less benevolent spirits could move between realms. To confuse these spirits, Irish Celts would dress in horrid disguises and leave offerings of food on their doorsteps to appease the sinister figures.

While we can't guarantee any Fae or spirits will visit you when in Ireland, their ancient abodes are plentiful throughout the country.

Fairy forts are said to be home to Fae of folklore called Sidhe, who lived beneath hills, within stone circles, or in other ancient circular dwellings, such as ancient Celtic ringforts called raths. Fairy forts were seen as escape routes when the Fae were driven underground by medieval Milesian settlers, and disturbing a fairy fort or building upon one can bring great harm and bad luck to the trespasser. So while they can be found in the thousands throughout Ireland, ensure you visit them with the appropriate amount of respect.

As for more traditional spooky spots, plenty of structures throughout Ireland are said to be home to human spirits and hauntings. Leap Castle in County Offaly usually tops most-haunted lists and is part of the county's "Haunted Triangle" of castles, which also includes those of Kinnitty and Charleville.

What remains of the Leamaneh Castle in County Clare is thought to be haunted by the ghost of Mary MacMahon. Known as "Red Mary," MacMahon was rumored to marry and then kill men once she no longer had use for them. She is said to have died of starvation after being tied to a tree, and she now allegedly haunts the grounds.

If you want to visit a luxurious castle with a dash of haunting, Cabra Castle Hotel in County Cavan is recommended. Visitors have reported all manners of supernatural events, from odd noises to floating objects to full-on apparitions, including a baby wailing on the steps of the castle at night.

These are only a few of the spots rumored to be haunted in Ireland—others include former prisons and asylums, graveyards, battlefields, and dozens of additional castles throughout the country. Chances are anywhere you travel in Ireland, you won't have to search far for a haunting tale.

PARIS, FRANCE

The City of Lights is central to the plot of *Tomb Raider: The Angel of Darkness* (2003). Lara Croft is chased through the rainy city streets of Paris after being framed for murder, spelunks through an ornate graveyard, scales scaffolding at an empty Parisian nightclub, and breaks into the famous Louvre for some after-hours viewing.

For a great taste of daily life, we suggest taking a more leisurely stroll through the Parisian streets. You can choose to meander at your own pace, or sign up for one of the many guided walking tours of Paris's famous neighborhoods. You can also tailor tours to your tastes, such as a culinary tour, a wine tour, or a street art tour. Some of the best walking tours in Paris are actually free, aside from the expected tip for your guide as a thank-you for the wealth of knowledge they've shared.

If cemeteries are of interest to you, we recommend a walk through the sprawling Cimetière du Père-Lachaise. Equal parts park and necropolis, it is the final resting place of many famous figures, including Frédéric Chopin, Jim Morrison, and Oscar Wilde. In it you'll see stunning examples of a variety of funerary practices, from small gothic graves to imposing baroque mausoleums.

Paris at night offers a wide array of entertainment, and while the Serpent Rouge isn't a real location, nightclubs are scattered across Paris. Districts like Le Marais and the Bastille offer both classy clubs and dive bars, depending on your mood.

As for Lara's excursion into the Louvre—the world's largest art museum—don't have your heart set on behind-the-scenes access unless you are an accredited researcher or scholar. However, it's nearly impossible to visit the Louvre and leave feeling disappointed. The museum is so much more than the *Mona Lisa*, although she is certainly worth a stop on your tour. Set in the stunning Louvre Palace, it is home to hundreds of thousands of objects, with over thirty-five thousand pieces on display, including textiles, jewelry, paintings, sculptures, and furniture. Between the permanent collection and rotating exhibitions, there is always something new to see within its walls.

For those unable to visit Paris, you can register for impressive virtual tours with behind-the-scenes access and Q&A opportunities—a great chance to get a taste of the famous collection.

As a major tourist destination, the Louvre will always be bustling with people. However, if you're open to an after-hours tour on Wednesday and Friday evenings, there will be less of a crowd. Note that the Louvre is closed on Tuesdays for weekly museum maintenance.

PRAGUE, CZECH REPUBLIC

Upon arriving in Prague from Paris in *Tomb Raider: The Angel of Darkness* (2003), Lara greets the city by saying, "Another cold, dark city. Great!" In reality, Prague is a city of warmth, even in the winter. The capital of the Czech Republic, Prague is also the historical capital of Bohemia, the largest of the three Czech historical regions.

We recommend a summer visit if possible, as that's when you can best explore the city streets and many bridges at a leisurely pace. The most famous of these bridges is the Charles Bridge on the Vltava River, which unites Prague Castle with Old Town. Lined with beautiful statues, the wide pedestrian path is frequently home to local artists and craftspeople exhibiting their work.

Old Town Prague features wonders like the five-hundred-year-old Astronomical Clock, the stunning Baroque Library in the historic Clementinum complex, and marvelous examples of Gothic and Baroque architecture.

If you're following in Lara's footsteps, you've got one more stop on your itinerary: the Strahov Fortress. On the opposite side of the Vltava River, it's actually a monastery founded in the mid-twelfth century. While still home to monks, there are many areas available to tour in the monastery. Highlights include the Theological Hall and Philosophical Library, both of which are decorated with opulent Baroque ceilings. While on the west side of the river, also check out St. Vitus Cathedral and Prague Castle. The latter is home to the Kohl's Fountain courtyard, which may look familiar to fans.

If you do visit in the winter, there is still much to experience in Prague. Old Town and Prague Castle are illuminated with holiday lights, squares are converted to Christmas markets or skating rinks, and the streets are full during local celebrations such as St. Nicholas Eve. You can also warm up in the many museums, restaurants, and pubs.

JAN MAYEN ISLAND/ARCTIC CIRCLE, NORWAY

In classic Tomb Raider fashion, Lara arrives at the Arctic Circle in *Tomb Raider: Underworld* (2008) by motorcycle, blows a hole in the ice with C4, and then dives into the shark-infested subzero waters below with only a wetsuit and rebreather.

Jan Mayen Island is a mostly desolate volcanic island of interest primarily to researchers, so tourists should consider visiting some of the Arctic Circle's more welcoming regions. Northern Norway is full of forests, fjords, and mountains and has exceptional views of the Northern Lights. The landscape is perfect for winter activities such as dog sledding, skiing, and winter kayaking. You can even stay the night in Snowhotel Kirkenes or visit the Lofotr Viking Museum on the

island of Vestvågøya. Arctic Norway is accessible by air, land, or sea via the various Norwegian coast cruises.

Greenland is also a great option for an Arctic Circle getaway. While it is on the North American continent, it is considered an autonomous territory in the Kingdom of Denmark. Greenland is also a better source of well-preserved Norse ruins than Jan Mayen Island. If you're determined to find the legendary Midgard Serpent, you'll have better luck at the timeworn farmstead of Eystribyggð in Hvalsey. Meaning "Whale Island," Hvalsey is also a popular tourist destination due to Fjord Church, the oldest Viking ruin in Greenland.

No matter where you're headed in the Arctic Circle, research is key to a safe and responsible trip. Smaller tours are less disruptive to the environment, wildlife, and indigenous inhabitants such as the Inuit population in Greenland and the Sami people in Norway. Wildlife highlights include whales, polar bears, reindeer, walruses, and the mystical narwhal.

Despite the freezing climate, the Arctic Circle sun reflects off the surrounding ice and can cause rapid sunburns, so dress appropriately and regularly apply environmentally conscious sunscreen to your exposed skin.

MEDITERRANEAN SEA

Almost completely landlocked, the Mediterranean Sea connects to the Atlantic Ocean via the Strait of Gibraltar. Its massive coastline touches countries across Europe, Africa, and Asia, making it a vital hub for travel and trade throughout documented history. It's no wonder that many civilizationals of note, such as ancient Egypt, Greece, and Rome, built around its waters.

The Mediterranean has claimed ill-fated vessels and even entire coastal cities due to natural disasters, weather, and warfare. Lara traverses the wreck of the *Maria Doria* in *Tomb Raider II* (1997), located in the Adriatic branch of the Mediterranean. The underwater adventure was heavily Inspired by James Cameron's *Titanic*, which released in theaters the same year. However, its name hearkens to the stunning *SS Andrea Doria*, which sank off the northeast coast of the United States in 1956 after colliding with another passenger liner.

Lara visits the Mediterranean Sea again in *Tomb Raider: Underworld* (2008), where she uncovers forgotten Norse ruins. While the inclusion of intact Norse structures in the Mediterranean is a narrative liberty of the game, there is much to see under the sea's surface.

Sometimes called Italy's Atlantis, the Baiae Underwater Park near Naples is a spectacular site. Once an ancient Roman resort, the city was ransacked, abandoned, and eventually sunk due to changes in the volcanic landscape. The phenomenon is called "bradyseism" and indicates a change in the elevation of a localized area due to the filling or emptying of subsurface magma chambers or other hydrothermal activity. Much of the ruins of Baiae are now thirty feet below sea level; they are shallow enough to make them accessible via glass-bottomed boat, snorkeling, and scuba diving, where you can float above ornate mosaic floors, intact statuary, and resting columns.

Antirhodos Island sank to the bottom of Egypt's Alexandria harbor when an earthquake shattered its foundation. It was only in the mid-1990s that "Cleopatra's Sunken Palace" was explored once more, with the most well-preserved pieces taken to local museums. There are still enough structures and items of interest to make it a site worth seeing, however. Scuba-diving tours are available to see the ruins up close.

If you're looking for a more modern *Maria Doria*-like experience, the wreck of the HMHS *Britannic* is unparalleled. The transatlantic passenger liner was the third White Star Line Olympic-class ship, alongside the *Olympic* and *Titanic*. The *Britannic* met an untimely end during World War I while in use as a hospital ship after striking a German naval mine. In the mid-1970s, the wreck was located by Jacques Cousteau near the Greek island of Kea. It only recently became an approved destination for divers, but the four-hundred-foot depth requires extensive experience and technical skill. The *Britannic* is one of ninety submerged wrecks Greece lifted diving restrictions on in March 2021, so there are many shallower options available for those working their way up to the big leagues.

Thank you to our European travel guide and recipe consultants: Eric Folliot; Laurie Scudder-Walker of Survivor Reborn; JoJo Neto of Lara's Backpack; Lauryl Zenobi; Kristina Horner; Andreas Theoharis; Jaclyn Trahanas; Dimitra Chartofylax; Olimpia Pagni; Roberto Pecorari; Alexandru Ciuta of Tomb Raider Drawings; Liz Leo; Tina Branigan; Steven Lynch; Erin Bower; Lindsay Weir; Katrina Hamilton; Hedi-Alexandre of Tombeau Croft; Kilian-Paul of Laraider; Jirka Ludvar, Aneta Ransdorfová, and JiĐí Kokavec of Lady Croft CZ; David Zimmermann; Diane Zimmermann; Ida Vesterelv; Rino / Raid Al Kadi of The Raider; Ahmad AlKaabi of Tomb Raider Arabia

EUROPEAN CUISINE
CHOCOLATE BARS

| **LOCATION:** EUROPE | **YIELD:** 3 CHOCOLATE BARS (MORE OR LESS, DEPENDING ON THE MOLD USED) | **DIFFICULTY RATING:** 2 OUT OF 3 |

Chocolate bars dominate the confectionary scene throughout Europe. This homemade recipe will make you a legend among your friends, family, and fellow travelers alike. Chocolate bars even give Lara a boost of energy in Tomb Raider: The Angel of Darkness *(2003), where they were used as health items. We suggest you proclaim, "I feel stronger now," after each bite.*

RECIPE ORIGINS

While everything chocolate can be traced back to Mesoamerica and the cacao seed, chocolate as a powder was first produced in 1828. Coenraad Johannes van Houten of the Netherlands developed a machine that allowed a press to separate cocoa butter from the cacao seeds, resulting in a pure chocolate powder. This led to the manufacturing of the first-ever solid chocolate bar in 1847, and the term "chocolate" became synonymous with the solid form, rather than its liquid ancestor.

COOK TIME: 30 MINUTES

INACTIVE TIME: 90 MINUTES

TOOLS NEEDED: Double boiler, or two pots to stack on top of each other, Small saucepot, Piping bag or plastic sandwich bag, Chocolate bar mold with deep cavities (to look similar to Lara Croft's chocolate bars, look for one that features long, thin chocolate bars with breakable sections), Blue-foil candy bar wrappers

INGREDIENTS:

12 ounces good-quality milk chocolate

⅓ cup heavy cream

1 cup chocolate hazelnut spread

DIRECTIONS:

1. Melt the chocolate in a double boiler. If you don't have a double boiler, fill a pot with an inch of water and place a similar-sized pot on top of that one. Place the chocolate inside the top pot and heat the pots over high heat. The water boiling in the bottom pot will produce steam, melting the chocolate in the top pot. Pour the melted chocolate into the chocolate bar mold. Move the mold around, spreading the melted chocolate across all available surfaces. Pour out any excess chocolate and reserve. Place the mold in the refrigerator to harden.

2. To make the ganache filling: Bring the heavy cream to a simmer in a small saucepot, then turn off the heat. Mix in the chocolate hazelnut spread. Move to a small bowl, cover with plastic wrap, and cool in the refrigerator for 30 minutes.

3. Place the ganache in a piping bag or a sealable sandwich bag with a corner cut off.

4. Remove the chocolate mold from the refrigerator. Pipe the ganache into each cavity in the chocolate molds, stopping just before the top.

5. Melt the remaining excess chocolate again in the double boiler, and fill the chocolate molds to the top. Place back in the refrigerator until solid (at least 1 hour).

6. Take the chocolate bars out of the mold and wrap them in the blue-foil wrappers.

BRITISH CUISINE
BEANS ON TOAST

| **LOCATION:** SURREY, ENGLAND | **YIELD:** 4 SERVINGS | **DIFFICULTY RATING:** 2 OUT OF 3 |

Quick and hearty, beans on toast are a favorite for people on the go. Most people will tell you British baked beans from a can are the only way to go, but if you don't have access to them, you can make your own version from scratch and fancy it up with some shredded cheese.

Beans on toast happens to be classic Lara's favorite meal, as noted in her original bio from 1996. The preparation provided for this teatime dish is for a more complex and posh experience, while traditionally the meal is as simple as the name implies.

RECIPE ORIGINS

Although bean dishes such as beans and bacon date back to medieval England, baked beans originate from indigenous American cuisine and were adopted by English colonists during the seventeenth century. Prominent in the New England region of the United States, baked beans spread throughout the world over the preceding centuries until beans on toast eventually became a classic breakfast meal in the United Kingdom.

PREP TIME: 5 MINUTES   **COOK TIME:** 25 MINUTES

TOOLS NEEDED: Medium Pot, Toaster

INGREDIENTS:

1 cup vegetable broth

⅓ cup ketchup

2 tablespoons light brown sugar, packed

2 tablespoons tomato paste

1 tablespoon apple cider vinegar

½ tablespoon Worcestershire sauce

1 teaspoon kosher salt

½ teaspoon garlic powder

½ teaspoon onion powder

½ teaspoon black pepper

2 (14-ounce) cans navy, cannellini, or other medium white beans, rinsed and drained

1 tablespoon cornstarch

¼ cup water

4 slices thick white bread

4 tablespoons (¼ cup) salted butter

1 cup cheddar cheese, shredded

DIRECTIONS:

1. Place vegetable broth, ketchup, brown sugar, tomato paste, vinegar, Worcestershire sauce, salt, garlic powder, onion powder, and black pepper in a medium pot, and stir. Mix in the beans, and bring the pot to a boil.

2. Lower the heat to medium low, and simmer for 20 minutes uncovered, stirring occasionally.

3. Mix the cornstarch with the water, and pour into the pot while stirring. Cook for an additional 2 minutes or until sauce is thick.

4. Toast and butter your bread, and spoon the baked beans on top. Sprinkle on some cheddar cheese.

LOCATION FEATURED IN:
Rise of the Tomb Raider (2015)

KEY LOCATIONS:
Croft Manor

ESSENTIAL EQUIPMENT:
Discovering Amelia's Tomb

BRITISH CUISINE
CHICKEN TIKKA MASALA

| ◔ **LOCATION:** LONDON, ENGLAND | ▤ **YIELD:** 4 SERVINGS | ♨ **DIFFICULTY RATING:** 2 OUT OF 3 |

Chicken tikka masala is a combination of chicken tikka (roasted chicken chunks) and curry sauce. The creamy dish is a global sensation, including in the United States and the United Kingdom, far from the Indian birthplace of its two main components.

Note that yellow onions in this recipe may be more commonly known as brown onions depending on your region.

RECIPE ORIGINS

Although commonly thought of as an Indian dish, chicken tikka masala may have originated from the South Asian community in Great Britain. Because of this, it's regarded as one of the first widely accepted examples of fusion cuisine. It's one of the most popular dishes in the United Kingdom, with multiple sources claiming ownership over its creation. It is believed to be a relatively new dish, however, as food critics and historians place its debut around the 1960s or early 1970s.

Due to the rapid explosion of curry's popularity across the world around the same time, the more likely explanation is parallel invention, where two or more entities independent of each other create essentially identical products. This is backed by a 1998 survey in the *Real Curry Restaurant Guide*, in which forty-eight different recipes for chicken tikka masala shared only a primary common ingredient: chicken.

🕐 **PREP TIME:** 10 MINUTES   🕐 **COOK TIME:** 40 MINUTES   🕐 **INACTIVE TIME:** 1 HOUR

TOOLS NEEDED: Large bowl, 2 large sauté pans, Immersion blender or standard blender

INGREDIENTS:

CHICKEN TIKKA (MARINADE):

1 cup plain yogurt

½ tablespoon kosher salt

2 teaspoons ginger-garlic paste (or 1 teaspoon grated ginger and 1 teaspoon grated garlic)

2 teaspoons garam masala

2 teaspoons turmeric

1 teaspoon black pepper

2 pounds boneless, skinless chicken breasts (or thighs, if you prefer), cut into 1-inch chunks

3 tablespoons vegetable oil, for cooking

MASALA (SAUCE):

2 tablespoons ghee

2 tablespoons ginger-garlic paste (or 1 tablespoon grated ginger and 1 tablespoon grated garlic)

1 yellow onion, diced

1 teaspoon garam masala

1 teaspoon cumin

1 teaspoon paprika

1 teaspoon turmeric

1 teaspoon coriander

1 teaspoon chili powder

1 teaspoon kosher salt

1 (14.5-ounce) can diced tomatoes

1 cup water

1 teaspoon granulated sugar

½ cup heavy cream

2 tablespoons chopped cilantro, plus more for topping

1 tablespoon lemon juice

Basmati rice, for serving

Naan, for serving

LOCATION FEATURED IN:
Tomb Raider III (1998)

KEY LOCATION:
City

MEMORABLE MOMENT:
Taking on Sophia Leigh

Continued on page 60

Continued from page 59

DIRECTIONS:

1. Mix together the yogurt, salt, ginger-garlic paste, garam masala, turmeric, and black pepper in a medium bowl. Add the chicken, coating thoroughly. Cover the bowl with plastic wrap and refrigerate for at least 1 hour, and up to overnight.

2. To make the masala: Heat the ghee in a large sauté pan over medium-high heat, and add the ginger-garlic paste and onion. Cook until the onions are soft, translucent, and beginning to brown, about 3 minutes.

3. Add the garam masala, cumin, paprika, turmeric, coriander, chili powder, and salt, and cook for another minute, stirring to coat the onions.

4. Add the diced tomatoes, water, and sugar. Bring to a boil, and then reduce the heat to a simmer. Let simmer for 10 minutes, then turn off the heat.

5. While the sauce is simmering, heat the vegetable oil in a large sauté pan on high heat. Add the marinated chicken. If it won't all fit in the pan at once, cook it in batches (to avoid overcrowding). Sear the chicken by cooking it for 3 minutes, then flip it over to the opposite side and cook for another 3 minutes.

6. Using an immersion blender, puree the sauce until smooth. If you don't have an immersion blender, carefully transfer the sauce to a blender, puree, then place back in the pan. Put the heat back on to medium-high.

7. Add the seared chicken, heavy cream, and 2 tablespoons of cilantro to the sauce. Simmer for 10 minutes, or until the chicken is cooked through. Stir in the lemon juice.

8. Plate the chicken tikka masala over basmati rice and top with a sprinkling of cilantro. Serve with naan.

JAFFA CAKES

| **LOCATION:** LONDON, ENGLAND | **YIELD:** 9 CAKES | **DIFFICULTY RATING:** 2 OUT OF 3 |

Jaffa cakes now come in all shapes and flavors, but the classic variety is a circular genoise (Italian sponge cake) base with a tangerine jelly filling topped with a chocolate coating.

Jaffa cakes are some of the United Kingdom's best-selling treats, and one of Lara Croft's favorite foods in the survivor trilogy. But the question is: Are they actually cakes, or are they biscuits (aka cookies)? This was a hotly debated topic especially in the early 1990s, when the manufacturer of Jaffa cakes argued in court that—despite their similarities to biscuits—they were, in fact, cakes. The court ruled in their favor, thus allowing Jaffa cakes to be taxed less, whereas biscuits are taxed more.

RECIPE ORIGINS

Jaffa cakes were created by the Scottish biscuit company McVitie & Price in 1927. The treats are named after Jaffa oranges, from which their jelly flavor is derived.

PREP TIME: 5 MINUTES   **COOK TIME:** 30 MINUTES   **INACTIVE TIME:** 1 HOUR

TOOLS NEEDED: Small pot, 9-by-13-inch casserole dish, 2-inch biscuit cutter or shot glass, 12-hole bun or muffin tin, Double boiler (or microwave-safe bowl)

INGREDIENTS:

JELLY:

¾ cup orange juice

¼ cup granulated sugar

Zest of 1 small orange

2 (¼-ounce) envelopes of unflavored gelatin

CAKE:

Unsalted butter, for greasing tin

1 large egg

¼ cup granulated sugar

¼ cup all-purpose flour

¼ teaspoon baking powder

⅛ teaspoon kosher salt

1 cup semisweet chocolate chips

LOCATION FEATURED IN:
Rise of the Tomb Raider (2015)

KEY LOCATION:
Lara's Apartment

MEMORABLE MOMENT:
Anna's Debut

DIRECTIONS:

1. To make the jelly, mix the orange juice, sugar, and orange zest in a small pot, and simmer over medium heat for 2 to 3 minutes, or until the sugar has dissolved. Sprinkle in the gelatin while mixing, continuing to mix until fully incorporated. Pour the jelly into a 9-by-13-inch casserole dish and refrigerate for at least 1 hour, or until firm.

2. Preheat the oven to 350°F, and grease the bottom and sides of the bun or muffin tin. Set aside.

3. In a medium bowl, whisk together the egg and sugar for 5 minutes, until light and fluffy. In a separate bowl, mix together the flour, baking powder, and salt, and then fold the flour mixture into the egg/sugar mixture.

4. Pour a tablespoon of batter into 9 cups of the prepared tin. Bake for 8 to 10 minutes, or until a toothpick inserted into one of the cakes comes out clean. Remove from the oven and let cool in the tin for 5 minutes, and then move to a wire rack. (If cakes are stuck in the tins, loosen them carefully with a butter knife.) Allow to cool completely, at least 15 minutes.

5. Take the jelly from the refrigerator and cut 12 rounds using the biscuit cutter or the top of a shot glass (you want each round to be slightly smaller than the cakes). Place one round in the middle of each mini cake.

6. Melt the chocolate chips in a double boiler or microwave, stirring every 30 seconds. Allow to cool slightly so it's thick but still liquid, and then pour over each cake, covering the top. Scrape the tines of a fork over the top, creating a crisscross pattern in the chocolate. Let cool 30 minutes, or until the chocolate has hardened.

FISH AND CHIPS

| **LOCATION:** DOVER, ENGLAND | **YIELD:** 4 SERVINGS | **DIFFICULTY RATING:** 2 OUT OF 3 |

The iconic British meal made of fried-battered fish and thick-cut fries is served at over ten thousand dedicated fish and chip shops (also called "chippies") throughout the United Kingdom. Now popular the world over, varieties of white fish are most commonly used, and garnishes vary from salt, vinegar, and fresh lemon in Britain and Ireland to tartar sauce in the US.

RECIPE ORIGINS

Chips and fried fish were both common foods in the United Kingdom for decades before the earliest known fish and chip shops. Fish fried in batter is believed to have been brought to the United Kingdom by Jewish immigrants as early as the sixteenth century; a similar dish called pescado frito was used to preserve the fish so it could be eaten the next day. The first dedicated fish and chip shop opened in London during the mid-nineteenth century. Within half a century, an estimated twenty-five thousand fish and chip shops existed across the UK according to the BBC, though that number decreased by over 50 percent by 2009, a full century later.

PREP TIME: 70 MINUTES   **COOK TIME:** 30 MINUTES

TOOLS NEEDED: Medium bowl, Deep pot or Dutch oven, for frying, Kitchen thermometer, Wire rack

1½ cups all-purpose flour, divided

3 teaspoons kosher salt, divided

1 teaspoon baking powder

1 cup cold dark beer (or seltzer water)

4 russet potatoes

Vegetable oil, for frying

1½ pounds cod (or other white fish) fillets

1 teaspoon black pepper

½ teaspoon paprika

Malt vinegar

1 lemon, cut into wedges, for serving

Tartar sauce, for serving

LOCATION FEATURED IN:
Tomb Raider III:
The Lost Artifact (2000)

KEY LOCATION:
Shakespeare Cliff

SECRET ENEMIES:
Pteranodons

DIRECTIONS:

1. To make the batter for the fish: Mix together 1 cup of flour, 1 teaspoon of salt, baking powder, and beer (or seltzer water) in a medium bowl. Whisk together until the batter is smooth and the consistency of pancake batter. If it's too thick, slowly add in more beer and mix. Set aside.

2. To make the fries: Peel the potatoes and cut them into ½-inch strips. Soak the potatoes in cold water for at least 1 hour, then rinse and pat dry.

3. Heat 3 inches of vegetable oil in a large, heavy pot to 325°F. Using a slotted spoon, place some of the fries in (enough where they are fully submerged and not overcrowded). Cook the fries for 5 to 6 minutes, then remove and set them on a paper towel–lined plate. Continue with the rest of the fries.

4. Heat the oil up to 400°F, and cook each batch of fries a second time until they are crisp and golden brown, about 5 minutes. Set on a paper towel–lined plate, salt to taste, and set aside.

5. Add another cup of oil to the pot, and bring the temperature down to 350°F.

6. Cut the cod fillets into 4 equal-sized parts. Pat the fish dry with a paper towel.

7. Place ½ cup flour, 1 teaspoon salt, black pepper, and paprika on a large plate and lightly mix the ingredients together. Dredge the fish fillets in the flour mixture, and then gently drop them into the batter.

8. Place the battered fish into the pot of oil, and fry for 7 minutes, flipping them over halfway through.

9. Move the fish to a wire rack to drain for a moment, and then plate with the fries. Sprinkle malt vinegar on the fish, and serve with a wedge of lemon and some tartar sauce.

BANGERS AND MASH

| **LOCATION:** LONDON, ENGLAND | **YIELD:** 4 SERVINGS | **DIFFICULTY RATING:** 1 OUT OF 3 |

Sausages, commonly known in the United Kingdom as bangers, and mashed potatoes is one of the British Isles' quintessential comfort meals. The bangers are traditionally made from beef, lamb, or pork and topped with onion gravy, though vegetarian options are slowly becoming increasingly popular.

RECIPE ORIGINS

The term "bangers" refers to the method in which the sausages were cooked during World War I. Due to meat shortages, the sausage casings were sometimes filled with water, leading them to explode during the cooking process.

PREP TIME: 5 MINUTES   **COOK TIME:** 45 MINUTES

TOOLS NEEDED: Stockpot, Large pan

INGREDIENTS:

MASH:

2½ pounds (about 8) Yukon Gold potatoes, peeled and quartered

4 tablespoons (¼ cup) salted butter

¾ cup whole milk

1 teaspoon kosher salt, plus more salt and black pepper, to taste

BANGERS:

1 tablespoon salted butter

8 pork sausages

ONION GRAVY:

2 tablespoons salted butter

1 large yellow onion, halved and sliced thin

2 tablespoons all-purpose flour

2 cups beef broth

½ teaspoon kosher salt, plus more to taste

¼ teaspoon black pepper, plus more to taste

DIRECTIONS:

1. Melt 1 tablespoon butter in a large pan on medium-high heat and place the sausages in. Let cook, turning often, for about 15 minutes, or until the sausages are browned all over. Place the sausages aside.

2. To make the gravy, turn the heat down to medium, add an additional 2 tablespoons butter to the pan, and then add the onion, coating it in the melted butter. Let cook for 10 minutes, until the onions are soft, translucent, golden, and starting to caramelize.

3. Mix the flour into the onions, and then slowly add the beef broth, salt, and pepper, bringing it to a simmer. Simmer for 8 minutes, stirring often, until the gravy has thickened. Add additional salt and pepper to taste. Place the sausages back into the gravy and keep the heat on low, allowing everything to stay warm while you make the mash.

4. Place the potatoes in a large stockpot and cover with water. Cover the pot with the lid, and bring to a boil. Lower heat to a simmer and let cook for 10 minutes or until the potatoes are easily pierced with a fork.

5. Drain the potatoes and return them to the pot. Add the butter, milk, and salt. Mash, combining the butter and milk while doing so. Salt and pepper to taste.

6. Divide the mash between 4 plates, top each with two bangers, and then pour a large scoop of gravy over the bangers.

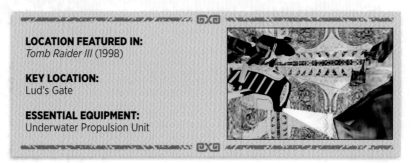

LOCATION FEATURED IN:
Tomb Raider III (1998)

KEY LOCATION:
Lud's Gate

ESSENTIAL EQUIPMENT:
Underwater Propulsion Unit

GREEK CUISINE
SPANAKOPITA

| **LOCATION:** UNDISCLOSED, GREECE | **YIELD:** 6 SPANAKOPITA SPIRALS | **DIFFICULTY RATING:** 2 OUT OF 3 |

This savory Greek pie is traditionally filled with spinach and feta cheese. Vegan versions, which remove any egg or dairy, are prepared for religious feasts such as Easter. Handheld versions, like these spirals, can often be found at Greek delis and bakeries and are perfect for eating on the go.

RECIPE ORIGINS

Modern spanakopita originates from the Espirus region in northwest Greece, possibly during the Ottoman Empire (1299–1922 CE). However, the dish is believed to stem from cheese pies wrapped in fig leaves and served at banquets in ancient Greece.

PREP TIME: 10 MINUTES

COOK TIME: 80 MINUTES

TOOLS NEEDED: Colander, Mixing bowl, Damp kitchen towel, Basting brush, Parchment paper–covered baking sheet

INGREDIENTS:

1 (16-ounce) package frozen chopped spinach, thawed

3 eggs, beaten together

10 ounces (about 2 cups) crumbled feta cheese

1 cup ricotta

3 green onions, thinly sliced

2 teaspoons fresh minced oregano

2 teaspoons fresh minced dill

½ teaspoon kosher salt

¼ teaspoon black pepper

1½ cups salted butter, melted, divided

1 (16-ounce) package (18 sheets) phyllo dough, defrosted

LOCATION FEATURED IN:
Tomb Raider (1996),
Tomb Raider: Anniversary (2007)

KEY LOCATION:
Midas's Palace

MEMORABLE MOMENTS:
Accidentally (or intentionally) turning Lara to gold

DIRECTIONS:

1. Preheat the oven to 375°F.

2. To make the filling, drain the spinach by squeezing it in a colander, removing as much liquid as possible.

3. Place the drained spinach in a large mixing bowl with the eggs, feta, ricotta, green onions, oregano, dill, salt, and pepper. Mix together.

4. On a flat workspace, lay out one sheet of phyllo dough with the longer side facing you. Place a damp kitchen towel over the rest of the phyllo dough to prevent it from drying out.

5. Carefully brush the phyllo dough with melted butter (phyllo can tear easily!). Top with another layer of phyllo dough. Brush that layer with butter and place one more layer of phyllo dough on top, for a total of three layers.

6. Spoon ½ cup of filling along the long side of the dough, an inch from the edge closest to you. Form it into a thin line, about ½ inch wide.

7. Fold the inch of dough closest to you over the filling, and then proceed to roll the dough tightly away from you. Once you form it into a log, work it into a spiral.

8. Carefully transfer the spiral to a parchment paper–covered rimmed baking sheet, and repeat steps 3–7 with the rest of the package. You should be able to make 6 spirals.

9. Brush the tops of the spirals with more melted butter, and bake in an oven for 55 to 60 minutes, or until golden brown, crunchy, and the spiral can maintain its shape when held.

ITALIAN CUISINE
BURANELLI

Venetian butter cookies are sugary treats known for their backward "S" shape, often paired with wine or dipped in coffee. The crunchy snack is a delicious holdover while exploring the streets and shops of Venice.

RECIPE ORIGINS

To native Italians, Venetian butter cookies are known as buranelli and originate from the Venetian island of Burano for which they were named. While the S-shaped style is the most popular, especially among tourists, O-shaped buranelli are also common.

🕐 **COOK TIME:** 30 MINUTES   🕐 **INACTIVE TIME:** 20 MINUTES

TOOLS NEEDED: Stand mixer, Spatula, Baking sheet, Parchment paper

INGREDIENTS:

8 tablespoons (½ cup) unsalted butter

½ cup granulated sugar

4 egg yolks

1½ teaspoons vanilla extract

1 teaspoon lemon zest

2 cups all-purpose flour

¾ teaspoon kosher salt

DIRECTIONS:

1. Preheat the oven to 375°F.

2. Place the butter and sugar in a medium mixing bowl. Mix for 10 minutes on medium-high, stopping every few minutes to scrape the sides of the bowl with a spatula.

3. Add the egg yolks to the mixer, one at a time, mixing for 1 minute in between each yolk. Scrape the sides of the bowl with a spatula.

4. Add the vanilla extract and lemon zest. Mix for 30 seconds.

5. In a small bowl, mix the flour and salt together, and then slowly add it into the butter and sugar mixture while mixing on low. Stop as soon as the flour is incorporated.

6. Cover the bowl and refrigerate for 20 minutes.

7. Divide the dough into 20 equal portions, and roll each one out into a thin log, then form the log into a backward "S" shape. Place the cookies on a parchment paper–covered baking sheet.

8. Bake for 10 minutes, or until the edges of the cookies begin to get golden brown.

9. Move to a wire cooling rack.

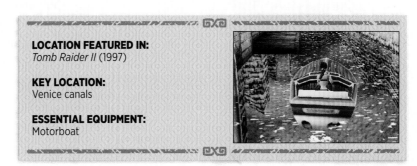

LOCATION FEATURED IN:
Tomb Raider II (1997)

KEY LOCATION:
Venice canals

ESSENTIAL EQUIPMENT:
Motorboat

FOCACCIA ROMANA

LOCATION: ROME, ITALY | **YIELD:** 1 BREAD | **DIFFICULTY RATING:** 2 OUT OF 3

Sometimes known as "pizza bianca," focaccia is a flat oven-baked bread similar to pizza and served as a side or sandwich bread. Like pizza, focaccia has a multitude of variations, with both sweet and savory toppings, or is served plain aside from a brush of rosemary and olive oil.

RECIPE ORIGINS

The first recorded appearance of the word "focaccia" was in 1300 CE, though Italian flatbreads predate that period considerably. In certain areas of northern Italy, variants of focaccia are traditionally prepared during Easter.

PREP TIME: 5 MINUTES   **COOK TIME:** 35 MINUTES   **INACTIVE TIME:** 90 MINUTES

TOOLS NEEDED: Stand mixer with a dough hook, Kitchen towel, Rolling pin, Basting brush

INGREDIENTS:

1 (2¼ teaspoons) packet active dry yeast

1 tablespoon granulated sugar

1½ cups lukewarm water

4 cups all-purpose flour, plus additional for dusting

¼ cup olive oil, plus 2 tablespoons for topping, and additional for greasing

1 tablespoon kosher salt

2 to 4 cloves garlic, minced

¾ tablespoon flake salt, for topping

½ tablespoon rosemary, for topping

½ pound mortadella or bologna, sliced (optional)

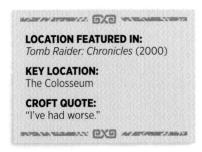

LOCATION FEATURED IN:
Tomb Raider: Chronicles (2000)

KEY LOCATION:
The Colosseum

CROFT QUOTE:
"I've had worse."

DIRECTIONS:

1. Combine the yeast, sugar, and warm water in a large mixing bowl. Let stand 10 minutes, or until foamy.

2. Add the flour, olive oil, and kosher salt to the bowl. Mix with a dough hook attachment, slowly at first, and then on medium speed once the flour is incorporated. Mix for 5 minutes, or until it forms a sticky dough. If you don't have a mixer, mix the dough together by hand and then knead it on a floured surface for 5 minutes.

3. Move the dough into a large oiled bowl and cover with a damp towel. Let sit in a warm location for 1 hour, or until the dough has doubled in size.

4. Transfer the dough to a floured surface and use a floured rolling pin or your hands to shape into a large rectangle approximately ½-inch thick and 8 by 14 inches in size. Cover the dough with a damp towel and let rise for 20 minutes.

5. While waiting for it to rise, preheat the oven to 400°F.

6. Transfer the dough to a greased baking sheet and poke deep indents into the bread with your finger (all the way to the bottom without creating a hole). Mix the minced garlic into 2 tablespoons of olive oil. Brush the olive oil and garlic mixture along the surface of the bread, allowing it to pool in the indents. Sprinkle with flake salt and rosemary.

7. Bake the bread for 20 minutes, or until the dough is evenly golden and a tap on the bottom of the loaf sounds hollow.

8. Let cool slightly for a few minutes, then cut into squares and eat while still warm, or slice in half width-wise and add thin slices of mortadella or bologna to make a pizza e mortazza.

Once you've perfected the bread, experiment with toppings: Try thinly sliced onions, tomatoes, or olives, or cover it with some tomato sauce and cheese.

IRISH CUISINE
IRISH STEW

| **LOCATION:** BLACK ISLE, IRELAND | **YIELD:** 4 SERVINGS | **DIFFICULTY RATING:** 2 OUT OF 3 |

While this Irish national dish features several specific ingredients, it's likely that every Irish mammy has their own take on the traditional recipe. Irish stew is made from water, mutton or lamb, and root vegetables such as potatoes and onions. This Irish dish is served around the world as a hearty and comforting easy-made stew, often with added ingredients such as carrots and various greens. While mutton or lamb are the traditional meats in this stew, you can also substitute the lamb with large chunks of beef stew meat. There are thousands of varieties of potatoes worldwide, so ensure you find a high-starch potato for this recipe.

RECIPE ORIGINS

Cauldrons were imported from Europe and became the predominant cooking tool in ancient Ireland. Meat and vegetables were readily available, but potatoes, which originated from South America, were not introduced until after the sixteenth-century Spanish conquest of Peru. Potatoes and stew became a staple of Irish cuisine, but the way in which potatoes were farmed led to widespread devastation during the Great Famine (1845–1849), resulting in over one million Irish deaths due primarily to starvation. The Great Famine, sometimes called the Irish Potato Famine or the Great Hunger, forever changed Ireland, and its effects are still felt throughout the country to this day.

PREP TIME: 10 MINUTES   **COOK TIME:** 2 HOURS, 10 MINUTES

TOOLS NEEDED: Medium bowl, Dutch oven or large pot

INGREDIENTS:

1 pound lamb stew meat, cut into 1-inch cubes

3 tablespoons all-purpose flour

2 tablespoons vegetable oil, divided

1 large yellow onion, roughly chopped

2 sprigs of fresh thyme

4 cups beef broth

6 large russet potatoes, peeled and cut into large chunks (1½–2 inches)

3 carrots, sliced into ½-inch-thick rounds

Salt and black pepper, to taste

Parsley, for garnish (optional)

DIRECTIONS:

1. Place the lamb pieces in a medium bowl and cover the meat with the flour. Mix together so all of the meat is evenly coated.

2. Heat 1 tablespoon of vegetable oil in a Dutch oven or large pot over medium-high heat. Add the lamb pieces and cook for 5 minutes, or until browned on all sides but not cooked through. Move the lamb to a plate and set aside.

3. Heat the other tablespoon of vegetable oil in the Dutch oven and add the chopped onion, cooking for 3 minutes or until browned.

4. Add the lamb, thyme sprigs, and beef broth. Scrape up any browned bits from the bottom of the pot, and mix everything together.

5. Bring to a boil, and then lower heat and simmer, covered, for 60 minutes.

6. Skim off any fat from the top with a cooking spoon and discard. Add the potatoes and carrots to the pot, mix, then cover and simmer for another 60 minutes or until everything is tender. Season to taste with salt and pepper.

7. Scoop into bowls, garnish each with a sprinkling of parsley, and serve with a large slice of buttered soda bread.

LOCATION FEATURED IN:
Tomb Raider: Chronicles (2000)

KEY LOCATION:
Labyrinth

CROFT QUOTE:
"Askgroth, Aquill, Aranqula, Belial, Bucom, Boliath . . . Help me!"

SCOTCH PIE

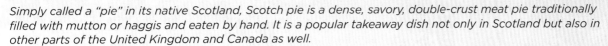

| **LOCATION:** SCOTTISH HIGHLANDS, SCOTLAND | **YIELD:** 8 PIES | **DIFFICULTY RATING:** 3 OUT OF 3 |

Simply called a "pie" in its native Scotland, Scotch pie is a dense, savory, double-crust meat pie traditionally filled with mutton or haggis and eaten by hand. It is a popular takeaway dish not only in Scotland but also in other parts of the United Kingdom and Canada as well.

Scotch pie uses a hot-water pastry, which can be difficult to work with. You have to work fast to get it rolled out, shaped, and pressed together before it cools off and dries out. If possible, try tackling this recipe with a partner to speed up the process.

RECIPE ORIGINS

Reportedly originating roughly five hundred years ago, Scotch pie was more commonly known as mutton pie. Today, both commercial manufacturers and citizens have differing recipes, including some designed specifically for throwing at sports events, either as part of the festivities (haggis hurling) or to show disdain for rival teams.

PREP TIME: 10 MINUTES   **COOK TIME:** 60 MINUTES

TOOLS NEEDED: Medium bowl, Medium saucepan, 8 large circular glasses, slightly under 4 inches in diameter, Parchment paper, cut into strips, Kitchen twine

INGREDIENTS:

FILLING:

1 pound ground mutton or lamb

½ teaspoon mace or nutmeg

½ teaspoon kosher salt

½ teaspoon black pepper

¼ cup beef stock

1 teaspoon cornstarch

DOUGH:

¾ cup water

½ cup shortening

4 tablespoons (¼ cup) salted butter

4 cups all-purpose flour

¼ cup milk, for glazing

TOPPING:

1 to 2 cups of gravy, mashed potatoes, or British baked beans for topping the pies (optional)

DIRECTIONS:

1. Preheat the oven to 350°F. Turn the glasses upside down and grease them with butter. Set aside.

2. Mix together the ground meat, mace or nutmeg, salt, and pepper. Refrigerate until needed.

3. To make the dough: Bring the water to a boil in a medium saucepan, and add the shortening and butter. Let melt, stirring frequently. Take off the heat.

4. Place the flour in a large bowl and make a well in the center. Pour the hot-water mixture into the middle and mix together with a spoon until it's no longer too hot to touch. Pour the dough onto a floured surface and knead until it fully comes together.

5. To shape the pies, you'll need to work quickly while the dough is still warm and pliable. (If it starts to harden too early, put it in the microwave for 10 seconds.) Separate a quarter of the dough and put it aside. For the rest of the dough, cut it into 8 equal parts and roll each one into a circle a little less than ¼-inch thick. Place each dough circle over the upside-down glasses, pressing down with your fingers to shape the dough fully around each glass. Place a strip of parchment paper around each dough-covered glass, and then tie twine around the dough. Carefully remove the dough (with the parchment paper and twine still on it) from the glass and turn it upright, forming little dough cups.

6. Roll out the bit of dough you set aside earlier, and use the top of one of the glasses to cut out 8 circles, slightly less than 4 inches in diameter. These will be the tops of your pies.

Continued on page 72

Continued from page 71

7. Take the filling out of the refrigerator and divide it into 8 equal balls. Place one in each pie, and gently press down on the meat, making sure it fills the bottom and leaves a gap near the top. Whisk the beef stock and cornstarch together in a small bowl, then pour ½ tablespoon of stock in each pie.

8. Place a top on each pie, sliding it down so the edges come up past the top. Lightly pinch the top with your fingers.

9. Move the pies to a baking sheet, cut a small steam hole in the middle of each top, and brush the tops of each pie with milk.

10. Bake for 45 minutes, or until the pies are firm and slightly browned.

11. Serve with gravy, mashed potatoes, or beans resting on the "shelf" on the top of the pie.

LOCATION FEATURED IN:
Tomb Raider III: The Lost Artifact (2000)

KEY LOCATION:
Willard's Lair

MAJOR ARTIFACT:
The Hand of Rathmore

NORWEGIAN CUISINE
POTATO LEFSE

| **LOCATION:** JAN MAYEN ISLAND, NORWAY | **YIELD:** 8 LEFSE | **DIFFICULTY RATING:** 2 OUT OF 3 |

Lefse is a traditional Norwegian flatbread made with potatoes or flour. Variations throughout Norway include thinner or thicker preparations and rolling the flatbread up with butter, sugar, and cinnamon, as is the case with our recipe. Potato lefse is often made with specialty tools—rolling pins, griddles, and pastry cloths explicitly made for the task of making lefse. But with a bit of patience and a lot of flour, they can be made with essential kitchen tools!

RECIPE ORIGINS

Potatoes were introduced to Norway around the mid-eighteenth century and became a staple of many dishes throughout the region. Lefse and potato lefse were commonly prepared and stored in large enough batches to last up to a year.

PREP TIME: 5 MINUTES   **COOK TIME:** 1 HOUR   **INACTIVE TIME:** 2 HOURS

TOOLS NEEDED: Large pot, Potato masher, ricer, or a fork, Rolling pin, Spatula, Griddle, Damp kitchen towel

INGREDIENTS:

2 pounds russet potatoes

¼ cup heavy cream

1 tablespoon unsalted butter, softened

1 tablespoon granulated sugar

1 teaspoon kosher salt

1 cup all-purpose flour, plus more for rolling out the dough

Salted butter and sugar, for topping

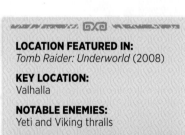

LOCATION FEATURED IN:
Tomb Raider: Underworld (2008)

KEY LOCATION:
Valhalla

NOTABLE ENEMIES:
Yeti and Viking thralls

DIRECTIONS:

1. Peel the potatoes and chop them into 1-inch chunks.

2. Place the potatoes in a large pot of boiling water, and boil for 10 to 12 minutes, or until they can be easily pierced with a fork.

3. Drain and mash the potatoes in a large bowl until they're completely smooth.

4. Add the cream, butter, sugar, and salt, and mix until the butter is melted and everything is fully combined. Refrigerate the bowl for 2 hours, or up to overnight.

5. Add the flour to the refrigerated potatoes, and mix with your hands, kneading it in until it feels like dough.

6. Divide the dough into 8 sections, and roll each into a ball.

7. Place a ball on a well-floured surface, and roll it out with a rolling pin until it's as thin as you can make it. Continue to flour the pin, surface, and dough as needed to prevent it from sticking.

8. Heat a griddle to 500°F and carefully move the lefse over to the griddle. (Try rolling it up onto the rolling pin, or flipping it onto a piece of parchment paper, then sliding it off the paper and onto the griddle.)

9. Cook for 90 seconds on each side, place the cooked lefse on a plate, and cover with a damp kitchen towel to prevent them from drying out.

10. Continue steps 7–9 with the other 7 sections.

11. Top each with lefse with butter and a teaspoon of sugar, and roll up.

FRENCH CUISINE
CRÊPES

| **LOCATION:** PARIS, FRANCE | **YIELD:** 5 CRÊPES | **DIFFICULTY RATING:** 2 OUT OF 3 |

Crêpes are super-thin pancakes served sweet or savory and as plain or as elaborate as one's imagination and culinary skills allow. Popular savory creations are as simple as Gruyère cheese, sliced ham, and egg. The versatility of crêpes is part of what makes them so popular across the world today. While the lemon and sugar in this recipe is a classic, feel free to experiment with your favorite fresh fruits, whipped cream, or chocolate hazelnut spread.

RECIPE ORIGINS

Crêpes are a descendant of ancient Greek tiganos, which mean "frying pan." In English, the word translates to "pan cake." The actual origin of modern-day crêpes is unknown, with French folklore pointing to a thirteenth-century housewife creating them by mistake in Brittany, the most Northwestern region of France and home to several of the world's oldest standing architectural sites. Regardless, crêpes have stood the test of time and are served worldwide, including in a wide range of specialized restaurants and street stalls known as crêperies.

COOK TIME: 15 MINUTES

INACTIVE TIME: 1 HOUR

TOOLS NEEDED: Stand mixer, 8-inch skillet or crêpe pan

INGREDIENTS:

CREPE:

½ cup all-purpose flour

¼ teaspoon kosher salt

2 eggs

½ cup milk

1 tablespoon granulated sugar

1 tablespoon unsalted butter, melted, plus more for cooking the crêpes

½ teaspoon vanilla extract

TOPPING:

1 lemon

5 teaspoons granulated sugar

LOCATION FEATURED IN:
*Tomb Raider:
The Angel of Darkness* (2003)

KEY LOCATION:
Le Serpent Rouge nightclub

MEMORABLE MOMENTS:
Exploring the Louvre

DIRECTIONS:

1. Mix the flour and salt together in a small bowl. Set aside.

2. Using a mixer, mix the eggs and milk together on low in a medium mixing bowl. Add the sugar, melted butter, and vanilla extract, and mix until combined.

3. Add the flour, and mix lightly until a batter forms. Cover the bowl with plastic wrap, and refrigerate for 1 hour.

4. Melt ½ tablespoon of unsalted butter on an 8-inch skillet or crêpe pan over medium heat.

5. Mix the batter and pour about 3 tablespoons onto the skillet, moving the skillet around to ensure the entire bottom is covered.

6. Cook for 1 minute or until the first side starts to brown, then flip with a large, flat turner, and cook for 20 seconds on the other side.

7. Move the crêpe to a plate and repeat steps 4–7 with the rest of the batter.

8. Squeeze some fresh lemon juice onto each crêpe and sprinkle with a teaspoon of sugar. Fold the crêpe in half, and then in half again. Give another quick sprinkle of lemon juice and sugar.

TRDELNÍK

I ⟨⟩ LOCATION: PRAGUE, CZECH REPUBLIC **I 🗄 YIELD:** 8 PASTRIES **I 🔥 DIFFICULTY RATING:** 2 OUT OF 3

Trdelník is a special type of treat known as a spit cake. Rolled dough is wrapped around a wooden stick or rolling pin–sized apparatus and then grilled over a spit. The grilled, hollow dough is traditionally topped with sugar and walnuts. Our recipe is a home version using cans or jars and your oven.

RECIPE ORIGINS

While spit cakes are believed to have originated in the mid-fifteenth century, trdelník dates back to roughly the mid-nineteenth century. The name is derived from the Czech-Slovak word "trdlo," which is the tool used during the cooking process. It is comparative to the Transylvanian spit cake kürtőskalács, and the following modern variant known as chimney cake and popularized in Prague is filled with ice cream.

PREP TIME: 5 MINUTES   **COOK TIME:** 40 MINUTES   **INACTIVE TIME:** 70 MINUTES

TOOLS NEEDED: Stand mixer, 8 empty 8-ounce mason jars or #300 tin cans (typically hold about 15 ounces), paper labels removed, Parchment paper, Baking sheet

INGREDIENTS:

DOUGH:

½ cup milk, lukewarm

1 (2¼ teaspoons) packet active dry yeast

3 tablespoons granulated sugar

4 tablespoons (¼ cup) salted butter, melted and slightly cooled

2 eggs

2½ cups all-purpose flour

ADDITIONAL INGREDIENTS:

1 egg, for egg wash

½ cup granulated sugar

¼ cup finely chopped walnuts

2 teaspoons cinnamon

Unsalted butter, cold, for greasing jars

LOCATION FEATURED IN:
*Tomb Raider:
The Angel of Darkness* (2003)

KEY LOCATION:
The Strahov Fortress

CROFT QUOTE:
"So, I guess it's up to me to stop you, then?"

DIRECTIONS:

1. Mix the lukewarm milk and yeast together in a medium mixing bowl. Let sit 10 minutes, or until the yeast is frothy.

2. Add the sugar, butter, eggs, and flour to the mixing bowl. Mix on low just until combined. Continue to mix on medium for 2 minutes.

3. Cover the bowl with a moist towel and let rest somewhere warm for 1 hour, or until the dough doubles in size.

4. While the dough is rising, preheat the oven to 400°F and prep the jars and the toppings. Grease the jars with butter and cover with parchment paper, then grease the paper with butter. Beat the egg in a small bowl for the egg wash, and mix the sugar, walnuts, and cinnamon together on a plate.

5. Divide the dough into 8 pieces, and roll each piece into a long rope, about 2 feet long.

6. Wrap a dough rope around each jar, allowing the dough layers to overlap slightly. Press the edges of the rope against the jar to help them stick.

7. Brush the wrapped dough in an egg wash and then roll it in the cinnamon/sugar/walnut mixture.

8. Place the dough-wrapped jars on a baking sheet, hole side down (so the dough isn't touching anything) and bake for 15 minutes, until the trdelník is golden.

9. Slide the trdelník off the jars and eat while warm. Trdelníks can be enjoyed as-is, or filled with whipped cream, ice cream, or chocolate hazelnut spread.

MEDITERRANEAN MEZZE PLATTER

LOCATION: MEDITERRANEAN SEA	**YIELD:** 3 DIPS	**DIFFICULTY RATING:** 1 OUT OF 3

Since the Mediterranean Sea touches countries across Europe, Africa, and Asia, there is no singular expression of Mediterranean food. However, the Mediterranean basin produces a specific climate, with mild temperatures and rain in the winter, and hot, dry summers. Such a climate has made three major crops popular in the region: wheat for breads and pastas, olives for their oil, and grapes for both drying and fermenting into wine. The cuisine differs substantially, paired with regional vegetables, fruits, meats, nuts, and spices.

Mezze platters are popular across the Mediterranean, consisting of small dishes, dips, and spreads, often paired with bread, veggies, and olives. They are great for grazing or a light meal.

RECIPE ORIGINS

Tzatziki: Variations of this cold yogurt dip are found throughout Greece, Turkey, the Balkan countries, and the Middle East. It is said to have roots in the Ottoman Empire (1299–1922 CE) through trade with India, when raita sauce was modified to soften its spicy nature. Since then, it has evolved and taken on a life of its own and is an essential dish in Greek cuisine. If you want an extra fresh addition to your tzatziki, it's common for Greeks to add a bit of spearmint to the mix.

Tyrokafteri: A spicy cheese spread originating from Greece, tyrokafteri varies from region to region but always has feta cheese at its core. Feta is a traditional Greek brined cheese from sheep's or goat's milk, white in color, and salty in taste. Feta is so well-known in Greece that it has a "Protected Designation of Origin" class in the European Union, meaning feta can only be branded on traditionally made cheese in select areas of Greece. A common addition to Greek tyroafteri is oregano, added to taste.

Hummus: The creation of hummus, a dip known throughout the world, is claimed by several countries in the Mediterranean region. It is most likely a Middle Eastern dish, as mentions date back as far as the thirteenth-century Bahri Dynasty of Egypt. The word "hummus" means "chickpea" in Arabic, which is its primary ingredient alongside tahini, garlic, and olive oil. A versatile dip, hummus is prepared in a variety of ways across regions and countries and is now a food enjoyed worldwide.

COOK TIME: 20 MINUTES

TOOLS NEEDED: Grater, 1 medium bowl, Food processor or blender, 3 small bowls

INGREDIENTS:

1 English cucumber

12 ounces plain Greek yogurt

2 tablespoons olive oil

1 tablespoon lemon juice

1 tablespoon minced garlic

½ teaspoon dill

Salt and black pepper, to taste

Additional dill, black pepper, or chopped parsley, for topping

TZATZIKI DIRECTIONS:

1. Peel and deseed the cucumber (cut the cucumber in half, then use a spoon to scoop out the soft seeded middle of the cucumber). Grate the cucumber into a small bowl, and squeeze out any excess liquid.

2. In a medium bowl, combine the grated cucumber, yogurt, olive oil, lemon juice, garlic, and dill. Mix and add salt and black pepper to taste.

3. Place in a bowl and top with a sprinkling of dill, black pepper, or parsley.

Continued on page 80

Continued from page 79

INGREDIENTS:

⅓ cup tahini

¼ cup lemon juice

2 cloves garlic, minced

2 tablespoons olive oil

½ teaspoon cumin

½ teaspoon kosher salt

1 (15-ounce) can chickpeas, rinsed and drained

1 to 2 tablespoons cold water, if needed

Olive oil, paprika, sumac, pine nuts, or chopped parsley, for topping

INGREDIENTS:

¼ cup olive oil

1 tablespoon red wine vinegar

1 red chili pepper, deseeded and minced

1 clove garlic

½ teaspoon red pepper flakes (add more or less depending on your personal spice level)

1 pound crumbled feta cheese

½ cup Greek yogurt

Olive oil and chopped parsley, for topping

HUMMUS DIRECTIONS:

4. Pour the tahini and lemon juice into a food processor or blender, and process for 1 minute or until light and whipped in appearance.

5. Add the garlic, olive oil, cumin, and salt, and process for 30 seconds. Scrape the bowl with a spatula and process for another 30 seconds.

6. Add the chickpeas and process for 2 minutes or until thick and smooth. If it's too thick, add a tablespoon of water to the mixture and process for another 30 seconds.

7. Place into a bowl and top with a drizzle of olive oil, a sprinkle of paprika or sumac, or a garnish of pine nuts or chopped parsley.

TYROKAFTERI DIRECTIONS:

8. Place the olive oil, vinegar, red chili pepper, garlic, and red pepper flakes in a blender or food processor. Process for 30 seconds, or until it's emulsified.

9. Place the crumbled feta, Greek yogurt, and the contents from the blender or food processor in a bowl. Mix thoroughly with a spoon.

10. Top with a small drizzle of olive oil and some chopped parsley.

LOCATION FEATURED IN:
Tomb Raider II (1997)

KEY LOCATION:
Wreck of the *Maria Doria*

NOTABLE ENEMIES:
Sharks

POST-EXPEDITION COCOA

| ◐ LOCATION: ARCTIC CIRCLE **| ◙ YIELD:** 6 SERVINGS **| ◊ DIFFICULTY RATING:** 1 OUT OF 3

Simple and rich, hot chocolate is the perfect way to warm up, whether it's after an Arctic expedition or bundled under your favorite blanket at home. This recipe makes a powdered cocoa mix that can be taken on an expedition. Once you've set up camp for the night, add hot water and enjoy! Not currently in the Arctic? Add the peppermint extract to feel a little "chill" while drinking.

RECIPE ORIGINS

Everything chocolate has an origin in Mesoamerica. The Mexica people saw cacao seeds as a gift from Quetzalcoatl, the god of wisdom. Cacao seeds were used as a form of currency throughout Mesoamerica and represented higher status among the Aztecs. Chocolate, or xocōlātl, was prepared as a bitter drink mixed with spices.

After the Spanish conquest, it is said that Hernán Cortés returned to Spain and introduced chocolate to Europe. The Spanish upper class adopted the bitter drink, and cocoa was even suitable for dowries between royals and aristocrats.

The bitter taste was replaced with a sweeter preparation, often adding vanilla and other spices, and became a luxury among European nobility. The first chocolate house, similar to a modern coffee shop, opened in 1657, though chocolate was still immensely expensive due to being imported from South America.

PREP TIME: 5 MINUTES   **COOK TIME:** 1 MINUTE

TOOLS NEEDED: Blender or food processor, Airtight container, Medium pot

INGREDIENTS:

¾ cup dry milk powder

½ cup powdered sugar

⅓ cup unsweetened cocoa powder

⅓ cup semisweet chocolate chips

Pinch of salt

6 cups hot water or milk, divided

Dash of peppermint extract

Marshmallows (optional)

Whipped cream (optional)

DIRECTIONS:

1. Place the dry milk powder, powdered sugar, cocoa powder, chocolate chips, and salt in a blender or food processor. Pulse until everything is mixed and forms a fine powder.

2. Store the mix in an airtight container.

3. To turn this into hot cocoa, mix ⅓ cup of the powder mix with 1 cup of hot water or milk in a mug. Add a dash of peppermint extract and top with marshmallows or whipped cream.

LOCATION FEATURED IN:
Tomb Raider: Underworld (2008)

KEY LOCATION:
Helheim

MEMORABLE MOMENTS:
Reuniting with Lara's mother

CHAPTER FOUR
ASIA & OCEANIA

◑ **KEY LOCATIONS:** Kolkata and Undisclosed, India; Undisclosed, China; Undisclosed, Tibet; Angkor Wat, Cambodia; Tokyo and Yamatai, Japan; Undisclosed, Kazakhstan; Undisclosed, Nepal; Undisclosed, Coastal Thailand; Undisclosed, Syria; Siberia and Barents Sea, Russia; Undisclosed, South Pacific

Key Terminology:

■ **Eastern Civilization/World:** A Eurocentric term used as a catchall for modern cultures throughout Asia with shared heritage, political systems, belief systems, and values with a strong foundational influence from early civilizations in India, China, and Japan. This is not a geographic term, as many countries located in central Asia such as Kazakhstan identify with the "Western World."

■ **Middle East:** A Eurocentric term used to describe a transcontinental region of Africa, Europe, and Asia, which generally includes all countries in the Arabian Peninsula (Saudi Arabia, the United Arab Emirates, Bahrain, Yemen, Oman, Kuwait, Qatar), Egypt, Turkey, Iraq, Israel, Jordan, Lebanon, Palestine, Syria, Iran, and several islands in the Mediterranean. The term "Greater Middle East" also tends to include additional North African countries, and Central Asian countries such as Afghanistan and Pakistan.

■ **Oceania:** A geographic term used to describe island chains of Australasia, Melanesia, Micronesia, and Polynesia.

■ **Pacific Islander:** A geographic and ethno-cultural term for the island inhabitants of Micronesia, Melanesia, and Polynesia.

■ **Aboriginal Australian:** A geographic and ethno-cultural term for the indigenous people of Australia and some of the surrounding islands.

With over four and a half billion people, approximately 60 percent of the entire world's population, Asia is the largest and most populated continent on our planet. China and India—each home to roughly 1.4 billion people—have long been global economic, religious, and political cornerstones. Asia is the birthplace of many of the world's dominant religions, including Christianity, Islam, Judaism, Hinduism, Buddhism, and Taoism, among many others.

Europe and Asia—separated solely by historical social constructs—are known collectively as Eurasia and may be considered a single continent in countries that use four-, five-, and six-continent maps. The Silk Road, a network of land and sea trade routes connecting Asia, Africa, and Europe, was vital to the expansion and commingling of both Eastern and Western cultures primarily from the second century BCE to the eighteenth century CE.

As hinted at by the various places Lara has ventured to throughout Asia, the land is made up of countless worlds within a world. From natural landscapes like Mount Everest to ancient human-made marvels such as Angkor Wat, there is no shortage of extraordinary sights to see. Numerous first civilizations originate from Asia, such as the ancient Liao, Huanghe, and Yangtze civilizations that developed the basis of Chinese civilization.

Asian linguistics are broken up into several major language groups, such as Afro-Asiatic languages that include Arabic, Aramaic, and Hebrew; Altaic language families including Koreanic, Japonic, and Turkic languages; and Sino-Tibetan languages that include Chinese and Tibetan, among countless others, some of which have long been extinct.

From the Great Wall of China in *Tomb Raider II* (1997) and *Lara Croft: Tomb Raider: The Cradle of Life* (2003) to the mystical island of Yamatai in *Tomb Raider* (2013), Lara's journeys have taken her to some of the most astonishing locales throughout Asia.

KOLKATA, INDIA

The opening cinematic of *Tomb Raider* (1996) shows Lara being propositioned for an expedition by mysterious businesswoman Jacqueline Natla during a quiet respite in a hotel in Kolkata, India.

Kolkata, the capital of West Bengal in northeast India, was officially renamed to Kolkata from Calcutta in 2001. More specifically, the name was changed back to its original Bengali pronunciation, with Calcutta being a relic of British rule. The entire region is an extraordinary amalgamation of British and Indian culture, both modern and historic.

This is best illustrated by two of Kolkata's most prevalent tourist attractions, Victoria Memorial Hall and Dakshineswar Kali Temple. Victoria Memorial Hall is a massive marble building erected in the early twentieth century with an Indo-Saracenic revivalist architectural style to pay tribute to the

first queen-empress of India, Queen Victoria. Dakshineswar Kali Temple is a Hindu temple built from the traditional architectural style of Bengal, known as navaratna. The two sites could not be more distinct from each other, and yet they are both equal parts of Kolkata and India's long, complex history. To get a taste of the multifaceted city, both are worth a visit.

Kalkota is a place of religious tolerance, peppered with noted places of worship, including the Cathedral of the Most Holy Rosary, the Beth-El Synagogue, the Kalighat temple to the goddess Kali, the Hindu temple of Birla Mandir, and the ornate Nakhoda Masjid mosque, among many, many others. The nearby Belur Math temple is an intentional blend of Buddhist, Hindu, Christian, and Islamic architecture and motifs as a symbol of unity.

There is also Kolkata's Mother House, where Mother Teresa was entombed after she died in 1997. The site is where she lived and served and is intentionally simple to reflect her modest lifestyle. A small on-site museum is home to some of her personal items, including her sandals, handwritten letters, and rosary.

The Indian Museum of Kolkata is a great way to learn about the country and its people. It is the oldest museum in the country, with a founding date of 1814, and one of the top ten oldest museums in the world. It boasts an array of collections that feature archaeology, anthropology, geology, zoology, botany, and Indian art, so you'll find everything from fossils and mummies to ancient armor, coin collections, and Mughal-era paintings.

UNDISCLOSED, INDIA

Far from the comforts of the museums and hotels of Kolkata, Lara explores jungles, temple ruins, and caves, and speeds along the coast of the Ganges River in *Tomb Raider III* (1998). This stage is notable for introducing the Quad Bike—a fan-favorite vehicle—which Lara uses to pursue a foe rafting down the river.

The Ganges—originally known as the Ganga River—stretches 1,600 miles from the Himalayas to the Bay of Bengal and is the third-largest river in the world after the Amazon and the Nile. The river has long been a vital part of Indian culture, politics, and livelihood. Many major cities were erected along the river's banks, and its source of water is instrumental to millions of residents. The

Ganges also has a profound spiritual meaning to the Indian people and is worshipped as Ganga, the goddess of purification. Pollution of the Ganges has become a problem in the past decade, but efforts to clean it up by the Indian government and NGOs around the world have begun to make progress in recent years.

Millions of Indians and tourists alike make pilgrimages to the Ganges to purify themselves in their waters, the most sacred being the Holy City of Varanasi. The labyrinthine city is one of the oldest inhabited cities in the world. The stone steps of the Dashashwamedh Ghat leading down to the river in Varanasi is also used as a site to spread ashes after ritual cremation of deceased loved one on nearby pyres. The hope is that releasing ashes into the Ganges will allow the deceased to reach Nirvana, ending the cycle of reincarnation. While you are welcome to watch these sacred rituals, photography of them is strictly prohibited.

If you want to explore ancient Indian ruins that would feel right at home in Tomb Raider, check out the Ellora Caves in the Aurangabad district of Maharashtra. The UNESCO World Heritage Site dates back to 600–1000 CE and is one of the largest rock-cut cave complexes in the world, nestled within an excavated basalt cliff. Around three of the one hundred caves in the complex are accessible to the public. Most of the cave structures are Hindu, but there are also Buddhist and Jain monuments at Ellora. All three are major religions born in India, highlighting the religious tolerance of ancient India. The Kailasa Temple in Ellora is one of the most astounding structures,

a megalith, carved from a single massive piece of stone over a period of one hundred years. The three-story monastery dedicated to Shiva is of particular importance to Buddhism.

Several hours north of Ellora you will find the Buddhist Ajanta caves, another World Heritage Site with thirty monuments carved into a crescent-shaped cliff. The cliffs were first thought to be carved between the second and first centuries BCE, beginning with simple dwellings and temples for its residents. More elaborate caves were added in the fifth and seventh centuries, featuring complex relief carvings, a twenty-foot reclining Buddha statue, and colorful paintings that are considered the best surviving example of ancient Indian Buddhist art. The caves were abandoned with the rise of Hinduism and reclaimed by the jungle for over a thousand years. Ellora and Ajanta are only two stunning examples of the many rock-cut complexes throughout India.

For a look at some of India's magnificent military architecture, the northwestern state of Rajasthan is home to over a hundred fortifications built into hills or mountains, with six particularly marvelous ones designated as the Hill Forts of Rajasthan by the UNESCO World Heritage Center. India is also home to dozens of national parks that give visitors a chance to see unique flora and fauna that cannot be found anywhere else in the world.

India is a massive subcontinent within Asia, and you could spend a lifetime exploring it. Be sure to prioritize what you most want to see and plan your city-hopping schedule well to sample what this incredible country has to offer.

UNDISCLOSED, CHINA

Tomb Raider II (1997) opens with Lara exploring the Great Wall of China in one of the franchise's most memorable set pieces. Among the many traps, dangers, and secrets hidden within the wall are two very hungry T. rexes.

Measuring over thirteen thousand miles in length, the Great Wall of China is a series of walls initially built during the Qin Dynasty (221–206 BCE) to protect against nomad incursions by connecting existing fortifications with walls of rammed earth and stones including granite. Later dynasties rebuilt and expanded the walls, with the modern-day remains primarily the efforts of the Ming Dynasty (1368–1644 CE), whose rule ended when the wall was breached by invading forces.

The Great Wall of China is now a popular tourist destination, with public transportation and guided tours regularly departing from Shanghai and Beijing. The tourist areas are typically well-preserved and maintained, but a great deal of the wall has deteriorated or been vandalized. Bricks from the wall are often stolen and sold despite being a serious crime given the wall's status as a World Heritage Site.

With thousands of miles to explore, choosing what portion of the Great Wall to visit can be daunting. There are two fantastic options outside of Beijing, each offering a slightly different experience. The Badaling section is considered the most representative of the wall—it is most in line with what you picture when daydreaming about a visit. Around fifty miles northwest of Beijing, this portion of the wall has been open to the public longer than any other—since 1957, to be exact. Ease of access is a key to Badaling's popularity—it's only a twenty-minute ride on the Badaling bullet train, which departs from the Beijing North Railway Station. Because Badaling is so popular with tourists, it also features the Great Wall Museum, as well as a variety of shopping and food options. You can access the wall via a vigorous hike or cable car to the top.

Badaling has a storied history, known as being the key strategic position and first line of defense on the pass to Beijing. There are interesting theories about the name too, tied to the number "eight," or "Ba." One theory asserts that this portion was built on the eight most dangerous mountain peaks in the area, resulting in eight construction leaders perishing. It is also said that after praying for support, the builders were then inspired to use eight different building techniques to complete it.

If you are looking for a quieter destination, however, we recommend visiting Mutianyu. It is a great example of restoration, including its twenty-three watchtowers. It's also the longest restored expanse of the wall that is open to visitors. Like Badaling, visitors can hike or take a cable car to the top, but if you're in the mood for a rush, you can take a toboggan back down. Mutianyu is also accessible for wheelchairs, which isn't always the case with ancient architecture.

Visiting the Great Wall is best when the weather is mild, from March through May or September through November. If you are hoping to avoid crowds, you'll also want to avoid major holidays in China or there will be a large number of domestic and foreign tourists joining you.

UNDISCLOSED, TIBET

Lara first visits Tibet in *Tomb Raider II* (1997) during her quest to find the magical Dagger of Xian. She explores the stunning southern foothills of the Himalayas, makes friends in a nearby monastery, and braves her way through a palace of ice.

For tourists traveling to Tibet, there are a number of unique challenges. Most importantly, independent travel to Tibet is forbidden by the Tibet Tourism Bureau. Foreign visitors are required to have a Chinese visa and Tibet entry permit and use qualified travel agencies such as tour guides. You must be accompanied by your Tibet guide at all times while visiting the museums, monasteries, and other points of interest. Additional permits are required when venturing outside Lhasa, the administrative capital of Tibet.

If all your paperwork is in order, however, you're in for scenery of a lifetime. Tibet is often referred to as "The Roof of the World," and Lhasa City is one of the highest cities in the world, located at an altitude of nearly twelve thousand feet above sea level. A large portion of Tibet is covered in the massive, mineral-rich Tibetan Plateau, which extends into India and China. Average elevation in the Tibetan Plateau is fourteen thousand feet, making it the world's highest plateau above sea level. The majority of the plateau is a dry steppe environment, but there are some grasslands on the periphery able to sustain livestock and nomadic inhabitants. The steppe is one of the least populated places in the world but is home to wolves, yaks, and the illusive and endangered snow leopard, among others.

While in the capital, check out one of Lhasa's most important stops, the sacred seventh-century Jokhang Temple. Originally known as the Tsuklakang (House of Religious Science), Johkang means "House of Buddha." To most of Tibet, it is the most revered of all their temples and houses a large golden statue of a young Jowo Shakyamuni Buddha, a sacred relic. The beautiful temple complex features Tibetan, Nepalese, and Indian vihara influences. Highlights include the main hall and courtyard, which is lined with different routes for pilgrims to turn prayer wheels. When visiting, you are welcome to light incense in dedicated places but are asked to dress modestly. Also be sure to ask permission to take photos of monks in residence or visiting pilgrims.

Nearby you can find the Potala Palace, a stunning fortified monastery situated on Red Hill. Visitors must climb a number of stairs at high altitude to reach it. The palace is a beautiful example of architecture common to Tibet and neighboring Bhutan. Previously used as the winter home to the Dalai Lamas until the 1951 annexation of Tibet by China, Potala Palace is now a museum and a UNESCO World Heritage Site. The massive complex features dozens of temples, office areas, dormitories, and more. The number of visitor tickets to the Potala Palace each day are limited, with many allocated to travel agencies. It is recommended you book your ticket through a tour, but you can wait in line the day prior to secure tickets if needed. Tours are limited to an hour within the complex, and you must abide by all customs, such as removing hats and sunglasses and wearing modest attire.

While you aren't likely to find Ski-Doos to zip through the nearby Himalayan foothills, Tibet has attractions and festivals worth seeing outside the city. The Nagqu Horse Racing Festival in August is full of amazing sights and sounds such as Tibetan opera, as well as horse racing, tug-of-war, wrestling, yak racing, and a glimpse into nomadic life. Tours from Lhasa make the festival accessible to tourists each year.

ANGKOR WAT, CAMBODIA

Cambodia holds a special place in Tomb Raider history. Not only is it the location where young Lara finds her iconic backpack—scavenged from a deceased adventurer who no longer needed it—a large portion of the 2001 film *Lara Croft: Tomb Raider* was filmed there. It was the first production to film in Cambodia in decades due to the long occupation and genocide at the hands of the Khmer Rouge.

Visiting Cambodia had a huge impact on Angelina Jolie, who plays Lara Croft in the film. She adopted her first child, Maddox, from Cambodia; became a special envoy for the United Nations High Commissioner for Refugees; and made the award-winning 2017 film *First They Killed My Father*, set during the Khmer Rouge rule. She now has dual US and Cambodian citizenship and purchased a large expanse of land near her home there to create a national wildlife reserve.

Cambodia is a sovereign state bordered by Thailand, Vietnam, and Laos in Southeast Asia. Tourism is second only to the country's textile industry in terms of economic importance, with Angkor Wat—the largest religious complex in the world—being the preeminent destination. The UNESCO World Heritage Site is a monolithic temple surrounded by a moat more than three miles long and an outer wall over two miles long.

The city of Angkor was the capital of the Khmer Empire, which expanded across much of Southeast Asia from the ninth through fifteenth centuries. The Khmer Empire consisted largely of adherents of Hinduism, followed by Buddhism. When originally constructed during the twelfth century as a mausoleum for King Suryavarman II, Angkor Wat was a Hindu complex dedicated to Vishnu. The Hindu influence on temple architecture can be seen throughout Cambodia as a result. By the end of the century, Angkor Wat had been converted to a Buddhist place of worship. Buddhism is now practiced by over 95 percent of the population in Cambodia.

At its height, the city of Angkor was a bustling city with a complex water distribution and storage system that is believed to have supported hundreds of thousands of people. Only religious buildings in the Angkor Empire were made from stone—often sandstone—so the commercial and domestic dwellings of Angkor have faded with time.

Travel to the Angkor Archeological Park, which contains Angkor Wat, along with dozens of other ancient Khmer Empire ruins, is possible by flying into Siem Reap, Cambodia's second-largest city, or you can travel by car or bus. From there, hiring a private tuk-tuk for the day can be an affordable option for transport between sites, or you can rent a bicycle for the day. Keep in mind that while Angkor Wat is often full of tourists, it's still an active and significant site of worship for many Buddhists.

A short distance away from the sprawling Angkor Wat is another temple worth visiting: Ta Prohm. Also a UNESCO World Heritage Site, the temple was made famous for its extensive screen time in the first Tomb Raider film. Locals are said to love Angelina Jolie and sometimes refer to Ta Prohm as the "Tomb Raider Temple."

The temple is in excellent condition and features beautiful reliefs of deities, monks, and guardian figures, but it is nature's reclamation of Ta Prohm that has made it most famous. Over the centuries trees have sprouted across the grounds, including on top of and across the stone structures. Their roots snake across the temple wherever they can find purchase, creating an otherworldly atmosphere irresistible to film crews and tourists alike.

TOKYO, JAPAN

Like Lara's visit to New York, her time in Tokyo in *Tomb Raider: Legend* (2006) is not of an archeological nature. She once again takes to the rooftops—though this time a little less discreetly. Her goal is to reach the penthouse of a Yakuza boss in possession of an artifact that is the key to solving her mother's disappearance many years prior. We don't recommend you follow Lara's lead and drive a Ducati along Tokyo's skyline. Instead, we suggest you take in the hundreds of culture, entertainment, and adventure options on the city's streets.

New York and Tokyo have much in common. Both are major metropolitan cities, with the Greater Tokyo area being the most populous metro area in the world. The Shibuya Crossing is Tokyo's equivalent of New York's Times Square, filled with grand displays of lights, technology, and shopping options. Unlike New York, however, Tokyo is Japan's political capital and home to the Emperor of Japan.

A destination for business and leisure alike, flights to Tokyo aren't hard to come by. Getting around in Tokyo is also famously tourist-friendly, made easy with the Yamanote Line train service. It loops through Tokyo's main urban spots—meaning if you miss your stop, you'll eventually end up where you need to be.

Shibuya is a great home-base option, as it offers accommodations from high-end hotels to economic capsule lodging for those who just need a place to sleep between activities. Primarily the commercial and financial center of Tokyo, Shibuya Crossing with its dazzling lights is something to behold—especially from above as thousands of pedestrians scramble across the streets with every green light.

As you leave Shibuya for the Yamanote Line, make sure to stop by the famous Hachiko Statue outside the Shibuya train station. The statue is a common meeting place and a monument to a loyal dog who met his owner at the station every day.

Be sure to stop at Harajuku Station while heading from Shibuya to Shinjuku. Harajuku is the epicenter of Tokyo youth culture and is excellent for seeing street fashion and picking up some ensembles of your own. Shinjuku is both the administrative hub for Tokyo's government as well as great for nightlife, especially for anyone interested in the popular Japanese pastime of karaoke. The Golden Gai area is famous for nightlife and bar hopping, with hundreds of small eateries to choose from. A short walk from the Golden Gai is the internationally known Robot Restaurant, where you can eat, drink, and witness a pop-culture show featuring a kaleidoscope of lights, performers, and animatronic wonders.

Another great stop on the Yamanote Line is Ueno, where you get some green time in Ueno Park. Especially beautiful when the cherry blossoms bloom in the spring, you can visit various shrines, temples, and Torii gates, or relax by ponds full of water lilies. Ueno is also home to many museums, such as the Tokyo Metropolitan Art Museum.

If you're feeling up for a quick train change, jump off the Yamanote Line and head to Asakusa Station about a mile away. Here you will be transported back in time with traditional foods and drinks and the breathtaking Sensō-ji Buddhist temple. It is Tokyo's oldest temple and features a five-story pagoda nearby.

Returning to the Yamanote Line as you circle back to Shibuya, gaming fans cannot miss a stop at Akihabara. Akihabara—also known as Electric Town—is a major shopping center and a pop-culture paradise. You can find everything electronics, video games, anime, manga, and virtually anything else Otaku culture—a Japanese term for people who have "consuming" interests. There are also mega arcades like the SEGA Game and Taito Centers where you can play both classic and modern titles, and the famous Super Potato shop is a great place to find rare gaming collectibles.

Surrounded by the many sights and sounds of the bustling city are some of the most fascinating and unique dining experiences you can imagine. Japan is renowned for its themed cafés, with themes ranging from monsters, Gundam, and kawaii maids to cafés filled with adorable cats and baby owls. Restaurants such as Ninja Akasaka employ modern-day ninjas to serve you in an Edo-style atmosphere, complete with dazzling illusions that would entertain even the most accomplished of world travelers.

Tokyo is a superb blend of antiquity and modernity unlike anywhere else in the world. You could easily spend countless weeks exploring the city, but there is much to see in the more remote parts of Japan as well.

YAMATAI, JAPAN

A young and inexperienced Lara finds herself shipwrecked on the mystical island of Yamatai in *Tomb Raider* (2013), isolated from the outside world by storms conjured by the shaman-queen Himiko. Yamatai as it appears in *Tomb Raider* (2013) is heavily inspired by folklore around the Dragon's Triangle, also known as the Devil's Sea. Located south of Tokyo in the Pacific Ocean, the area is subject to many superstitions, generated mainly by tales of missing ships and their crew during the mid-twentieth century. Fortunately for aspiring visitors, those urban legends have long been debunked.

Though believed to have been a real place and ruled over by the priest-queen Himiko, the exact location and details surrounding the kingdom of Yamatai have long been debated by historians and archeologists alike. Its location is particularly difficult to decipher since the only written accounts come from historical journals of Chinese diplomats.

Yamatai is thought to have existed in the second to third centuries during the Yayoi period of Japan. Two primary theories exist around its location: the "Kyūshū theory" and the "Kinai region theory." If you want to experience and weigh in on the debate yourself, both locations are south of Tokyo and a great way to see what Japan has to offer outside the metropolis area.

A mountainous region home to the most active volcano in Japan, Kyūshū is one of Japan's five main islands. Its proximity to the Korean peninsula has made it an important place for interactions between early Japanese inhabitants and those of mainland

Asia. The Kyūshū theory says that the Saga Prefecture in northern Kyūshū could be the location of Yamatai, primarily due to ruins found in the area.

Uncovered in the mid-1980s, the Yoshinogari Historical Park is a crucial site for Japanese history, with ruins in the settlement dating back to the Yayoi period associated with Himiko's rule. Archaeologists have uncovered around two thousand dwellings, burial mounds, food storehouses, and fortified buildings protected by multiple ditches or defensive walls. Many everyday artifacts such as mirrors, tools, and coins have been discovered. Artifacts from China and the nearby Korean peninsula area were also discovered. The park features many reconstructed Yayoi period dwellings for visitors to see, providing more context into how the people of the time lived.

While in Saga City, you should check out its namesake castle. Built in the early seventeenth century and reconstructed multiple times, it is now the largest reconstructed wooden castle in Japan. After your visit, you can explore the green oasis of the nearby Sagajo Park and visit the city's many pottery shops to see the craft Saga is renowned for. If you're open for some driving, Saga Prefecture's Takeo Onsen hot springs are said to have been in use for over a thousand years and are known for their curative powers.

The other rumored location of Yamatai is in the Nara Prefecture, once known as Japan's historical Yamato Province. Nara was once the capital of the ancient province of Kinai.

Much of the "Kinai region theory" is based on the discovery of a keyhole-shaped burial mound in Nara's Sakurai City, called the Hokenoyama Tomb. Carbon-dating the tomb puts it at the right time, and the bronze mirror found inside is said to be similar to one of the one hundred gifted to Himiko from the Chinese Wei Dynasty.

Nara is also known for the friendly wild sika deer that inhabit Nara Park near Mount Wakausa. The park also features several beautiful temples and gardens to explore. The Tōdai-ji Buddhist temple complex is the largest wooden structure in the world and houses a massive bronze statue of the Buddha. The stunning Shinto Kasuga Grand Shrine and Kōfuku-ji Buddhist temple are also located within the park. All of the structures, as well as others in Nara, are part of a UNESCO World Heritage site for the "Historic Monuments of Ancient Nara."

While in Nara, making a thirty-minute drive to Osaka is a great choice for many reasons, including to visit the Osaka Prefectural Museum of Yayoi Culture. The museum aims to educate about Yayoi life and has a beautiful exhibit and statue of Queen Himiko in it.

UNDISCLOSED, KAZAKHSTAN

Lara travels to the transcontinental Republic of Kazakhstan twice, once in *Tomb Raider: Legend* (2006) and again in the second *Tomb Raider* film, *Lara Croft: Tomb Raider: The Cradle of Life* (2003). Her visits mostly involve industrial buildings such as the secret laboratory housing Project Carbonek and the prison housing the mercenary Terry Sheridan, respectively. Since Lara's visits to Kazakhstan don't highlight the incredible history and natural beauty of Kazakhstan, we've offered up a full itinerary for fans who visit.

Kazakh philosophy is freedom under the endless sky, represented by the blue expanse of their national flag. Kazakhstan is the world's largest landlocked country, and one of the most sparsely populated, with no more than fifteen people per square mile. It has an extensive history of nomadic traditions in the endless steppe landscape, and a blending of cultures through trade along one of the branches of the Silk Road.

The largest city in Kazakhstan is Almaty, home to more than 10 percent of the country's total population. Kazakhstan is primarily comprised of Turkic peoples, a wide array of ethnic groups who can be found across Asia and Europe. The population is primarily Muslim, followed by Christian, with a very small Buddhist community. Formerly a part of the Soviet Union, both Kazakh and Russian are official languages of Kazakhstan.

While in Almaty, be sure to visit the Central State Museum, in which you could easily spend a day examining ancient artifacts, Turkic cultural objects, and natural curiosities. A replica of Kazakhstan's famous Golden Man—a warrior skeleton discovered with over four thousand golden ornaments and dated to somewhere between the fourth and third century BCE—can also be seen at the museum. The tsarist Russian Orthodox church known as the Ascension Cathedral in Almaty is also stunning, and a monument to the influence of Russia in the region.

If you're up for a half-day adventure in the nearby nature park, you can take a bus to Medeu Dam, climb the 842 steps to the top, and then jump on a cable car (or continue walking if you're up for the challenge) to the Chimbulak ski resort. The site offers amazing views of several local mountain peaks, and in hot months, an escape to a cooler climate. Locals also escape the summer heat by taking a beach weekend at the nearby Kapchagay Reservoir.

The massive expanse of virgin land stretching in all directions makes for stunning landscapes and parks. The Tian Shan mountain range is located near the Kazakh/Chinese border and is the birthplace of the 256-mile Charyn River, which travels through the Charyn Canyon. The canyon is referred to as the Valley of Castles for its unique natural rock formations and is just one of many stunning sights in Charyn National Park. A prime destination for seeing what natural beauty Kazakhstan has to offer, Charyn National Park is commonly accessed by way of bus from Almaty. It is a great getaway for hiking, fishing, and stargazing and is lauded for the unbelievably clear night skies.

For a bit of ancient Kazakh history, head to Turkistan City, about a ten-hour drive west from Almaty. The mausoleum of Khoja Ahmed Yasawi—a significant Turkic poet and Sufi who widely influenced the area—is a must-see. The mausoleum is a stunning example of Turkic architecture. Khoja Ahmed Yasawi was known for helping spread Islam throughout the region, and as such the country is dotted with beautiful historic Kazakh Muslim sites and ruins to explore. Ancient sites from various cultures can also be found along the Silk Road travel routes, which connected the East to the West with trade.

UNDISCLOSED, NEPAL

Nepal holds a critical and tragic place in Lara's history across all three timelines. In the original timeline, Lara survives a plane crash at the age of twenty-one and survives alone for two weeks in the frigid heights of the Himalayan Mountains. In the Legend timeline, a much younger Lara and her mother, Lady Amelia Croft, once again crash land in the Himalayas. And in the Survivor timeline, Amelia Croft dies from injuries sustained during a plane crash in the region.

In both the original and the Legend timelines, surviving the aftermath of the plane crash in the harsh climate of the Himalayas is instrumental in shaping Lara to be the toughened explorer she eventually becomes. There are many opportunities for safe adventure in Nepal, with Mount Everest calling to the world's most skilled and seasoned climbers.

The world's highest mountain looms over twenty-nine thousand feet above sea level. While the climb is not particularly technical, dangers such as avalanches, altitude sickness, and severe cold and wind make the ascent perilous even for physically fit climbers. Most climbers stop at one of the two base camps, each a little more than halfway up the mountain.

As Nepal did not allow foreigners to enter the country until 1951, the first recorded efforts to summit Everest were made through the north ridge approach on the Tibetan side. A 1924 expedition resulted in two mountaineers disappearing into the clouds. The body of one of them was discovered seventy-five years later, 2,250 feet from the summit. The second mountaineer's whereabouts are still unknown, presumably among the more than three hundred other lost souls to have perished on the mountain. Sherpa Tenzing Norgay and New Zealander Edmund Hillary were the first to summit Everest in 1953. The Sherpa people are an ethnic group native to the Himalayas of Nepal. They're known for having for exceptional mountaineering ability and expertise, particularly at high altitude. The term "Sherpa" has often been misused by foreigners and has been made synonymous with local climbing guides regardless of their ethnicity. Both Sherpas and porters—who carry equipment to camps on the mountain—are essential to the success of a climb.

Unless you are a veteran climber who has trained specifically for the challenges Mount Everest has to offer, we do not recommend giving it a go. If you are fixated on getting a taste of Everest, you can always hire a helicopter to take you to Everest Base Camp. That being said, Nepal has so much to offer in addition to its most famous peak.

Nepal is incredibly diverse and home to over one hundred unique ethnic groups across its various terrains. The compact capital city of Kathmandu is a must to visit, with residents known for their exceptional friendliness. There are many Hindu and Buddhist temples to see in the city, in addition to museums, and the famous Durbar Square in front of the old Royal Palace. Although structures in the square were damaged in a 2015 earthquake, it is still a beautiful and bustling site.

We think the best way to live like Lara in Nepal, however, is to get lost in the wilderness. Well, not actually lost, as you will need a trekking permit to hike in any of Nepal's national parks. The vastness and variety of Nepal's parks is impressive.

Chitwan National Park is a lowland jungle in the south known for having the best wildlife viewing in the country, and some say, in all of Asia. It is known for sightings of rare species such as the one-horned rhino, Bengal tiger, sloth bear, and gharial crocodile. Koshi Tappu Wildlife Reserve to the east is said to be a paradise for bird watchers, and Khaptad National Park to the west features vast expanses of green, rolling hills.

The parks to the north are a siren's song to hikers. The Annapurna Circuit is a sought-after adventure for more seasoned hikers, averaging eleven full days on your feet. It is said to be one of the best long-distance treks in the world, with the Himalayas always in view and offering the opportunity to visit remote Nepalese communities you wouldn't otherwise encounter. The best time for this hike is from the end of September to the end of November, after the heavy rains, known as the monsoon season. It is strongly recommended you hike in groups or with a tour guide, as the terrain and altitude are challenging, but like most of Nepal, the journey is unlike anything else in the world.

UNDISCLOSED, COASTAL THAILAND

In *Tomb Raider: Underworld* (2008), Lara descends into the mythical capital of the serpentine Naga by way of ancient Buddhist ruins on the coasts of Thailand. Later, Lara tracks down the antagonist's ship in the nearby Andaman Sea, where she confronts her longtime nemesis Jacqueline Natla.

Travel to the picturesque islands of Thailand usually starts in the beautiful and bustling metropolis of Bangkok. Some combination of buses, trains, air travel, and ferries will then allow you to hop between the mainland and key island destinations in the Andaman Sea, such as Phuket. Approximately ten million tourists visit Phuket annually and are a major contributor to the country's economy. As such, Phuket is a tropical paradise loaded with tourist attractions and luxury hotels.

While the lush greenery of Lara's coastal Thailand adventure is very much accurate, you won't usually find ruins like the ones she explored near Thailand's coasts. To check out examples of stunning Thai architecture throughout time, it is worth going inland to visit to the Old City of Ayutthaya. Accessible by bus or train from Bangkok, it's only a ninety-minute ride from the capital.

Ayutthaya is an important city to Thai history, founded in the fourteenth century and situated at the conjunction of three rivers that form an island—the Chao Phraya, Lopburi, and Pa Sak. The rivers connect to the sea but are inland enough to protect from naval warfare, resulting in a strategically placed hub for trade. The many canals of Ayutthaya have resulted in a nickname of "The Venice of the East," although that moniker has been shared with several other cities across Asia.

Ayutthaya was the capital of the Ayutthaya Kingdom. The kingdom rose to prominence with the decline of the Khmer Empire, which had spread its influence across several southeast Asian countries, including Thailand (then known as Siam). A hub for learning, art, and trade between the East and West, Ayutthaya flourished for some time. Both the city and empire eventually fell due to civil war and invasions from nearby Burma (now known as Myanmar) in the eighteenth century. After the city of Ayutthaya was destroyed, the seat of power was moved and eventually settled in Bangkok.

The city boasts dozens of sites worth seeing, so you should plan on at least two days to visit Ayutthaya island and outlying complexes. Many of the sites on the island are recognized as UNESCO World Heritage Sites for being beautiful examples of Ayutthaya architecture. Most of the Buddhist temples feature Prang or Chedi spires, which were adapted from and incorporated into their designs from regional influences like the Khmer Empire. Wat Yai Chai Mongkhon is one of the most famous and features a beautiful reclining Buddha statue. Wat Phra Si Sanphet features three stunning temples adorned with Chedis that soar into the sky. And don't forget to stop by Wat Mahathat, where the Head of the Buddha, a famous stone carving of Buddha's head being reclaimed by tree roots, can be found.

UNDISCLOSED, SYRIA

In an attempt to understand the supernatural events of Yamatai in *Tomb Raider* (2013), Lara returned to her father's research on immortality and picked up a lead in Syria. *Rise of the Tomb Raider* (2015) opens with Lara scaling a cliff in an undisclosed location in Syria, searching for the Tomb of the Eternal Prophet. Although the tomb she discovers is empty, it leads her on a quest to find the lost city of Kitezh, which she eventually uncovers in Siberia.

The region of Syria—also historically called Levant—is used to reference a geographical area comprised of Syria, Israel, Lebanon, Palestine, and Jordan, most of which boarder the Levantine Sea, the easternmost part of the Mediterranean Sea.

Part of the Fertile Crescent—created by the convergence of the Tigris and Euphrates Rivers—the area is a crossroads of northeast Africa, western Asia, the Arabian Peninsula, and the eastern Mediterranean. This has made the Syrian region vital to trade throughout history. It has also resulted in many foreign rulers and ruling empires including ancient Egyptians, Israelites, Babylonians, the Roman Empire, the Byzantine Empire, the Umayyad Caliphate, the Ottoman Empire, and many more. As such, ruins of note in the region often feature structures from many different cultures and religions.

Modern Syria is home to several of the oldest continuously inhabited cities in western Asia, including the City of Jasmine, Damascus, with carbon dating placing the site's founding around at least 6300 BCE, although it is thought to have been inhabited even earlier, from 10,000–8,000 BCE. Once visited by nearly nine million people annually, the Syrian civil war (2011–present) has resulted in staggering death and displacement figures and reduced tourism to near nonexistence. In addition, sadly many historical sites have been substantially damaged by the ongoing war. Restoration efforts are being made, including to UNESCO World Heritage Sites like the ancient ruins of Palmyra and the Old City of Aleppo.

As a safe alternative to Syria, consider a trip to Jordan, a neighboring country to the south that welcomes many tourists every year. While the Wadi Rum desert and the archaeological city of Petra are often what draw people to Jordan, the country also features expansive sites with ruins from the Syrian region.

When visiting Jordan, starting in the capital city of Amman is recommended, not only because of its proximity to the airport but also because it's home to a massive Roman amphitheater in the middle of the city. On top of the Jabal al-Qala'a hill, you can also find the remains of the Temple of Hercules and an Umayyad dynasty palace.

Heading north toward the Syrian border, you will find the city of Jerash, a blend of Greco-Roman and Levantine culture. Jerash is often considered one of the best examples of Roman ruins outside of Italy, and we suggest reserving at least a full day to walk the sprawling site. Highlights include a hippodrome, two amphitheaters, a colonnade, the nymphaeum, and temples to Zeus and Artemis, as well as newer additions of two churches and a mosque.

A bit farther north you will find the city of Irbid and the town of Umm Qais. The ruins and structures here are similar to those found in Jerash and equally exquisite.

South of Amman you'll find Umm ar-Rasas, which is known for the remains of sixteen Byzantine churches and incredibly well-preserved mosaics. It is believed there is much more left to uncover at the site.

There are dozens of other sites across Jordan you can visit to see these beautiful blends of architecture—but don't forget to also visit some of Jordan's other famous sites, including the Wadi Rum, Petra, and Ma'in Hot Springs, among others. We suggest ending your visit with a trip to a Dead Sea spa, as it is a great way to rest after all your adventures.

BARENTS SEA, RUSSIA

Adjacent to the Arctic Ocean, the Barents Sea is off the northern coast of Norway and Russia, with territorial waters divided between the two. Although the Barents Sea is part of the larger Arctic Ocean, it is warmer than you might expect due to the strong North Atlantic current, which also makes it fertile fishing grounds.

Honestly, most of Lara's adventures in the Barents Sea don't look fun—or legal—to replicate. Lara begins by infiltrating the Russian Zapadnaya Litsa naval base on the Kola Peninsula, before sneaking onto a nuclear submarine. She then takes an extreme-depth suit for a spin in search of the Spear of Destiny, thought to be lost in a German U-boat. It doesn't end well, with the nuclear sub joining the U-boat at the bottom of the sea.

Finding wrecked German vessels in the Barents Sea isn't out of the question, though, as it saw significant action during World War II. Most skirmishes were with German surface-dwelling ships rather than with submarines, however.

If you want to explore the regional naval history, head to the port city of Murmansk, Russia. It is the largest city in the Arctic Circle, with a peak of around three hundred thousand residents, although that number has declined over the past several decades. You can access Murmansk by car, train, or bus, but it's a nearly forty-hour train ride from Moscow. You can also fly or travel by sea from some Nordic cities.

Most tourist spots you'll find in Murmansk relate to its importance as a military stronghold in World War II, such as the Northern Fleet Naval Museum. Murmansk acted as an important supply distribution point for the Soviet Union and other Allied Powers but suffered extensive damage when attacked by German forces. It is one of a dozen cities in the Soviet Union to be awarded Hero City status for its heroism during World War II.

If you do feel like a frigid underwater adventure, ice diving is popular in the nearby White Sea. There you will find vast kelp forests, ice formations, soft corals, and loads of marine life. Ice diving requires more extensive experience than other forms of scuba diving, so it isn't an activity for beginners. Murmansk is also a great destination for winter sports and a popular location for viewing the Northern Lights.

SIBERIA, RUSSIA

Clues unearthed in Syria lead Lara Croft to Russia in *Rise of the Tomb Raider* (2015), where Lara spends the vast majority of her adventure in the Siberian wilderness. In the snowy landscape she survives death-defying mountain ascents and close encounters with wildlife, discovers a geothermal valley home to a recluse remnant civilization, and uncovers a lost byzantine city reclaimed by ice.

Despite being located entirely within Asia, Siberia is considered politically and culturally European as part of Russia. Siberia is one of the most sparsely populated regions in the world, accounting for 77 percent of Russia's land but only 23 percent of its total population. The region is known for its brutal winters, which reach -50 degrees Fahrenheit, but the Siberian summer is warm and welcoming.

Demographically, most residents of Siberia are of Slavic decent; however, there are several high-density areas for indigenous Siberians, including the Buryats and Yakuts, who speak Mongol and Turkic, respectively. The major city of Novosibirsk is an excellent assemblage of Siberian culture, with historic buildings, museums, and a world-renowned zoo that helps breed over thirty endangered species. Since Lara is known to love a good opera, we suggest you visit the Novosibirsk Opera and Ballet Theatre, a massive building with unique architecture built in the 1930s in the then-new Classic Empire style.

Since Lara doesn't shy away from educational opportunities, the Akademgorodok district of Novosibirsk is home to dozens of unique research institutes, including the Institute of Nuclear Physics, the Museum of Archaeology and Ethnography, and the Novosibirsk State University. Walking around the district is a breath of fresh air, as it was built inside an expansive cedar forest.

For a beautiful example of traditional Siberian architecture, you can visit the wooden houses of Tomsk, a five-to-six-hour drive north of Novosibirsk. One of the oldest cities in Siberia, Tomsk is dotted with ornate, colorful architecture that contrasts the snowy white landscapes in winter months. Much of Russia's architecture was influenced by Byzantine culture and features ornate mosaics, wood carvings, and floral patterns. Wood construction is also common due to the vast supply of timber found in Siberia, with brick or stone saved for larger communal buildings.

For a bit of action, the Siberian landscape is full of opportunities for outdoor adventures. Climbing Mount Belukha on the border of Kazakhstan is popular with mountaineers, and the mountain itself is considered a UNESCO World Heritage Site as part of the Golden Mountains of Altai.

Roughly one thousand miles east lies Lake Baikal. Sometimes called the Pearl of Siberia, the lake is a major attraction and another UNESCO World Heritage Site. It contains more than 20 percent of the world's fresh surface water, making it the largest freshwater lake in the world. It is also the deepest lake in the world and is renowned for its crystal-clear water, which then turns to magnificent blue crystal-clear ice. Depending on the season, various tourist activities are available on and around the lake, including ice diving, dog sledding, ice golfing, and ice rafting—on actual sheets of floating ice—in the winter.

Located equidistant between Novosibirsk and Lake Baikal is Stolby Nature Sanctuary and the nearby city of Krasnoyarsk, where you can find an array of lodging. Part of the Sayan Mountains, the park is known for dramatic rock complexes jutting from the earth like towers, a favorite for free climbers around the world.

Winters are long and summers are short in Siberia, so timing your trip around the warmer season is likely a good start for most travelers. The Trans-Siberian Railway, which runs 5,772 miles from Moscow to the Russian Far East, is the longest railway system in the world. For a truly epic adventure, riding the

Trans-Siberian Railway and planning a series of stops along the way will let you experience a wide array of popular and hidden destinations.

UNDISCLOSED, SOUTH PACIFIC

Lara's search for meteorite artifacts in *Tomb Raider III* (1998) takes her to the South Pacific, where she traverses through jungles with hidden waterfalls, kayaks through river rapids, and explores a coastal village. She also dodges crocodiles, narrowly escapes quicksand, and fends off dinosaurs—because this is Tomb Raider, after all. Eventually, she makes her way to the Temple of Puna, where she discovers one of

the meteorite artifacts—the Ora Dagger—is protected by a deity who can summon and control poisonous creatures called dragonettes.

Tourists will find the South Pacific, known for hospitality toward visitors, far more accommodating. The South Pacific broadly refers to the Pacific Ocean south of the equator. The Pacific Ocean expands from Asia and Australia in the west to the Americas in the east; the Arctic and Antarctic Oceans define its north and south borders. According to the *Encyclopedia Britannica*, the Pacific accounts for one-third of the entire planet's surface area, which is equivalent to more than all landmasses combined. It has twice as much water volume as the Atlantic and is home to the ocean floor's deepest discovered point—the Mariana Trench in the Philippine Sea—which descends over thirty-six thousand feet.

The Pacific Ocean is also home to the largest number of islands globally, which are often archipelagos with volcanic hot spots. The islands dotting the vastness of the Pacific Ocean were divided into three subregions in the 1830s by the French explorer Jules Dumont d'Urville, based on his studies of the geographic and ethnic divides. Still used today, the islands are grouped into Micronesia, Melanesia, and Polynesia.

Micronesia is located just north of the equator and includes six countries within four primary archipelagos: the Mariana Islands, Caroline Islands, Marshall Islands, and Gilbert Islands. The United States territory of Guam is a popular tourist destination in Micronesia, featuring both modern luxury resorts and an array of outdoor activities.

While Micronesians are considered Pacific Islanders, Melanesia and Polynesia are part of the actual South Pacific. Melanesia begins just south of Micronesia and is home to four autonomous countries: Papua New Guinea, the Solomon Islands, Vanuatu, and Fiji, along with various French-administered islands. Papua New Guinea is a stronghold of natural beauty with an agricultural population mostly isolated from the world.

Polynesia is the largest of the three subregions: a collection of over one thousand islands throughout the Central and South Pacific Ocean. Many Polynesian people share some common cultural practices and spiritual beliefs, and have related languages despite the vast distance between them. This is due in large part to the advanced wayfinding and boat-building techniques of Polynesian navigators, which aided them on long-distance voyages across the ocean.

Polynesia's geographical region, known as the Polynesian Triangle, stretches from Hawaii in the north all the way down to New Zealand in the south and extends to Easter Island in the east. A territory of Chile, Easter Island is most famous for its natural beauty and archaeological offerings. Over nine hundred Moai—human figures with oversized heads carved from stone—can be found throughout the island. Other large island groups include the Cook Islands, French Polynesia, Niue, Samoa, Tokelau, Tonga, Tuvalu, and Wallis and Futuna. From swimming in the crystal-blue waters of Bora Bora to watching the sunrise from above the clouds on the Haleakalā volcano summit in Maui or snorkeling along the coral reefs of Tahiti, the wondrous activities of Polynesia are endless.

It is never explicitly disclosed where in the South Pacific Lara visits in *Tomb Raider III* (1998). While Polynesian mythology does reference a historical figure by the name of Puna, a French line of Lara Croft

figures from 2005 ties the game to Fiji. This ambiguity just means you have plenty of options in your itinerary.

You can't go wrong with Fiji, the most popular tourist destination in the South Pacific. With over three hundred islands, you can choose to visit modern hot spots or explore off the beaten path. Island-hopping packages for Fiji are common, and you will need to move around to sample some of Fiji's main attractions.

The Coral Coast of Fiji is one of the most popular destinations, where you can snorkel, paddleboard, surf, enjoy lagoon cruises, and sample the many spas. Additional adventure awaits in jet-boat river safaris, roller-coaster zip rails, jungle waterslides, and Jet Skiing. You can view local wildlife by snorkeling with manta rays or booking shark encounters or dolphin-watching expeditions. You can walk through the jungle on elevated boardwalks for a more leisurely activity, enjoy mud pools and hot springs, explore Sigatoka Sand Dunes National Park, or visit the Garden of the Sleeping Giant, which boasts over two thousand varieties of orchids.

Booking a Fiji heritage and culture tour will take you to the Nakabuta Pottery Village to see the traditional craft. You can also partake in a nighttime celebration with local food, a kava ceremony—the national drink of Fiji—and a meke show, a traditional type of dance.

The South Pacific is incredibly diverse geographically, culturally, and politically, so you will have to narrow in on the type of experience you're looking for before selecting your island paradise of choice.

Thank you to our Asia & Oceania travel guide and recipe consultants: Satabdi Pulakanti; Akanksha Sachan; Yagnaseni Chowdhury; Chen JunJun of Tomb Raider China; Colin Smith; Ruby Wong; Makenzie Greenblatt; David Hudson; Yamamoto Daisuke; Leilan Nishi; Chris Parker; Tipwarong Tangadunrat; Christine Zakhour; Rhonda Miller; Rino and Raid Al Kadi of The Raider; Ahmad Alkaabi of Tomb Raider Arabia; Sergey Khoroshykh; Elijah Marlborn; Lucky Chanzlyn Aguon Jackson; Zachary Cohn; Jillian Wall; Candice McLaughlin

ASIAN CUISINE
CURRIED TRAIL MIX

| ◐ **LOCATION:** ASIA | 🗋 **YIELD:** 4 CUPS | 🔥 **DIFFICULTY RATING:** 1 OUT OF 3 |

A sweet and spicy snack packed with energizing nuts, curried trail mix is a great option whether you're hiking on the Great Wall of China, camping in the Himalayas, or simply taking the dog for a walk back home.

🕐 **PREP TIME:** 5 MINUTE   🕐 **COOK TIME:** 30 MINUTE

TOOLS NEEDED: Large bowl, Small saucepan, Rimmed baking sheet

INGREDIENTS:

1 cup cashews

1 cup almonds

1 cup peanuts

½ cup pistachios

½ cup dry roasted edamame

¼ cup coconut oil

¼ cup light brown sugar, packed

2 tablespoons curry powder

½ teaspoon cumin

A dash of cayenne pepper

½ teaspoon kosher salt

¼ cup coconut flakes

DIRECTIONS:

1. Preheat the oven to 300°F.

2. In a large bowl, combine the cashews, almonds, peanuts, pistachios, and edamame. Set aside.

3. Melt the coconut oil in a small saucepan over medium heat. Add the brown sugar, curry powder, cumin, cayenne pepper, and salt, and stir over medium heat for 1 to 2 minutes, or until it's mixed and fragrant.

4. Add the curry mixture to the nut mixture, and stir with a spatula to coat evenly.

5. Spread the trail mix out in a single layer on a parchment paper–lined rimmed baking sheet, and sprinkle with coconut flakes.

6. Bake for 25 to 30 minutes, mixing them once at the halfway mark. The trail mix will be browned once done.

7. Let cool and store in an airtight container.

KATI ROLL

| 🌐 **LOCATION:** KOLKATA, INDIA | 🍴 **YIELD:** 8 ROLLS | 🔥 **DIFFICULTY RATING:** 3 OUT OF 3 |

Kati translates to "stick" in the native Bengali language. The skewer-roasted kebab is wrapped in paratha or roti (Indian flatbread) and traditionally seasoned with coriander and served with egg or chicken. The popularity of kati rolls has led to widespread variations, including vegetarian options. While this is a nice vegetarian version, you can add chicken by marinating ½-inch cubes of chicken just as you would the paneer, then sautéing it with a tablespoon of oil until fully cooked. Add into the filling mixture the same time you would add the paneer.

RECIPE ORIGINS

Kati rolls were created around 1932 and are attributed to Nizam's, a restaurant in Kolkata, India. A combination of Nizam's two most popular dishes—kebabs and paratha bread—kati rolls would go on to become a regional sensation. The restaurant is still thriving to this day in Kolkata's New Market district.

⏱ **COOK TIME:** 45 MINUTES   ⏱ **INACTIVE TIME:** 1 HOUR

TOOLS NEEDED: 2 large bowls, Kitchen towel, Large pan, Blender or food processor, Parchment paper or aluminum foil

INGREDIENTS:

ROTI DOUGH:

2 cups atta or whole wheat flour

½ teaspoon kosher salt

1 tablespoon vegetable oil

¾ cup water

8 eggs, for cooking onto the roti

Ghee, for topping the roti

MARINADE:

2 tablespoons plain yogurt

1 teaspoon ginger-garlic paste
(or ½ teaspoon grated ginger and
½ teaspoon grated garlic)

1 teaspoon kosher salt

1 teaspoon Kashmiri chili powder
(or paprika with a touch of
cayenne pepper)

1 teaspoon garam masala

1 teaspoon kasuri methi
(fenugreek leaves)

¼ teaspoon turmeric

1 tablespoon lemon juice

1 pound paneer, cut into
½-inch pieces

CHUTNEY:

1 cup cilantro (known as coriander
in India)

¼ cup mint leaves

1 green chili, chopped

1 inch ginger, peeled and chopped

2 cloves garlic

2 tablespoons water

1 tablespoon lemon juice

½ teaspoon cumin

1 teaspoon sugar

1 teaspoon kosher salt

FILLING:

1 tablespoon vegetable oil

1 red onion, thinly sliced

1 green pepper, deseeded and sliced

1 large tomato, cut into thin wedges

ADDITIONAL INGREDIENTS:

½ cup cilantro, chopped

Continued on page 100

Continued from page 99

DIRECTIONS:

1. To make the roti dough: Combine the atta or wheat flour and salt in a large bowl, and add the oil and half the water. Start kneading the dough together, and slowly add in the rest of the water while kneading until a smooth dough is formed.

2. Cover the dough with a damp kitchen towel and set aside for 30 minutes.

3. While the dough is resting, marinate the paneer. In a medium mixing bowl, combine the yogurt, ginger-garlic paste, salt, chili powder, garam masala, kasuri methi, turmeric, lemon juice, and paneer, and mix until the paneer is coated. Refrigerate for 30 minutes.

4. To make the chutney: Combine cilantro, mint, chili, ginger, garlic, water, lemon juice, cumin, sugar, and salt in a blender or food processor, and blend until it forms a puree. Set aside.

5. Once the dough has rested, separate it into 8 small balls. Roll them out into thin circles, about 6 inches in diameter, on a floured surface.

6. Heat a tiny bit of vegetable oil on a large pan or griddle on medium-high heat. Cook the roti for 90 seconds on each side, or until little golden-brown spots appear. Remove the roti and bring the heat down to medium-low. Beat an egg and then pour the egg onto the pan or griddle and let cook for 30 seconds or until it starts to cook but isn't solid on the top. Place the cooked roti on top of the egg, adhering the egg and roti together. Brush ghee on top of the roti and cook for 2 minutes. Flip, and cook for another minute. Remove and repeat the process for the rest of the rotis.

7. To cook the filling: Remove the marinated paneer from the refrigerator. Heat a tablespoon of vegetable oil over medium-high heat in a large pan and add the onion, green pepper, and tomato. Sauté for 2 minutes. Add the paneer, and cook for 5 additional minutes, or until paneer is warmed, stirring often.

8. To assemble a kati roll, take a roti and spread the chutney across the egg side. Place ⅛ of the filling in the center, and top with 1 tablespoon of chopped cilantro. Roll the roti into a wrap shape, and wrap the bottom half with parchment paper or aluminum foil to keep it closed. Repeat with the rest of the ingredients.

LOCATION FEATURED IN:
Tomb Raider (1996)

KEY LOCATION:
Imperial Hotel

KEY QUOTE:
"What's a man gotta do to get that kind of attention from you?" —Larson Conway

INDIAN CUISINE
VADA PAV

Vada pav is a deep-fried potato dumpling encased in a bread bun. The vegetarian snack is native to the Indian state of Maharashtra, where it began as a popular street food and has since become a mainstay at restaurants across the country.

RECIPE ORIGINS

As with kati rolls, the creation of vada pav is widely attributed to a specific vendor. In this instance, Ashok Vaidya is believed to have had the first vada pav stall, positioned near Dadar railway station in 1966. The cheap and carb-heavy snack became a favorite of mill workers before spreading to the wider populace.

 PREP TIME: 5 MINUTES

 **COOK TIME:** 60 MINUTES

TOOLS NEEDED: Small pan, Blender or food processor, Large pot or Dutch oven, Kitchen thermometer, Potato masher, ricer, or a fork, Mortar and pestle or food processor, Large bowl, Whisk

INGREDIENTS:

DRY RED CHUTNEY:

6 cloves garlic

6 red chilies (mild ones)

½ cup dried coconut

½ teaspoon red chili powder

Kosher salt, to taste

POTATO VADA:

2 large russet potatoes

2 green chilis

6 cloves garlic

1 tablespoon vegetable oil

½ teaspoon mustard seeds

7 curry leaves (or fresh bay leaves)

⅛ teaspoon turmeric

2 tablespoons chopped cilantro

Kosher salt, to taste

VADA BATTER:

1 cup gram flour (also known as besan or chickpea flour)

⅛ teaspoon turmeric

½ cup water

Pinch of kosher salt

Pinch of baking soda

ADDITIONAL INGREDIENTS:

Oil for deep frying

8 green chilis, deseeded

8 pav or dinner rolls

Chutney (see recipe on page 99)

Tamarind chutney

LOCATION FEATURED IN:
Tomb Raider III (1998)

KEY LOCATION:
River Ganges

ESSENTIAL EQUIPMENT:
Quad Bike

Continued on page 104

Continued from page 103

1. To make the dry red chutney: Dry roast the garlic in a small pan for 2 minutes, or until they start to brown and soften. Add the red chilies and roast until crisp. Set the chili/garlic mixture aside on a paper towel–lined plate. Place the coconut in the pan, and cook for 2 minutes. Add the coconut, chili/garlic mixture, red chili powder, and a pinch of salt to a blender or food processor, and grind to make a coarse chutney. Set aside.

2. To make the potato vada: Peel the potatoes and chop them into 1-inch chunks.

3. Place potatoes in a large pot of boiling water, and boil for 10 to 12 minutes, or until they can be easily pierced with a fork.

4. Drain and mash the potatoes in a large bowl until they're completely smooth.

5. Cut the tops off the green chilis (and deseed if you want it a bit less spicy) and mash the pepper and garlic cloves in a mortar and pestle or blend in a food processor. Set aside.

6. Heat a tablespoon of oil in a small pan. Add the mustard seeds and cook until they start to crackle. Add in the curry leaves, and sauté for just a few seconds.

7. Add the chili/garlic mixture and the turmeric. Stir and cook for 1 minute, or until the garlic has softened and become less pungent.

8. Pour this mixture into the mashed potatoes. Add the cilantro and a pinch of salt, and mix until fully combined. Taste, and add additional salt if needed.

9. Roll the potato mixture into 8 equal-sized balls.

10. To make the vada batter: Whisk the gram flour, turmeric, cup water, salt, and baking soda together in a large bowl until it forms a batter the consistency of pancake batter. If it's too thick, add more water a tablespoon at a time.

11. Heat about 3 inches of oil to 375°F in a large pot or Dutch oven.

12. Dip the potato balls into the batter, fully coating them, and then drop gently into the oil. Fry, rotating once halfway through, for 3 minutes, or until golden brown. Remove from the oil and let drain on a paper towel–lined plate.

13. Once the fried vada is finished, place the additional green chilis in the hot oil, frying for 1 minute.

14. Slit the pav or dinner rolls in half, keeping them attached on one side, and spread the green chutney on one side and the tamarind chutney on the other. Spoon a small amount of dry red chutney on top. Place a fried vada in the center of each roll and include one fried green chili.

INDIAN CUISINE
MANGO LASSI

| **LOCATION:** UNDISCLOSED, INDIA | **YIELD:** 2 MANGO LASSIS | **DIFFICULTY RATING:** 1 OUT OF 3 |

Lassi is a popular Indian drink that blends dahi (yogurt) with water or milk, spices, and mint or fruit. When the drink is infused with liquid cannabis, it is known as bhang lassi. A similar and equally common drink using water for a thinner consistency is called chaas.

RECIPE ORIGINS

The origins of lassi have been difficult for historians to determine. Modern-day vendors sometimes refer to it as the "ancient smoothie," but verifiable details around its inception remain a mystery.

PREP TIME: 3 MINUTES

COOK TIME: 2 MINUTES

TOOLS NEEDED: Blender

INGREDIENTS:

1 cup mango, diced

1 cup plain yogurt

½ cup milk

2 tablespoons granulated sugar

¼ teaspoon cardamom

Crushed pistachios, optional garnish

Saffron strands, optional garnish

DIRECTIONS:

1. Place the mango, yogurt, milk, sugar, and cardamom in a blender, and puree for 30 seconds or until smooth.

2. Pour into two glasses and garnish with crushed pistachios or a couple of strands of saffron.

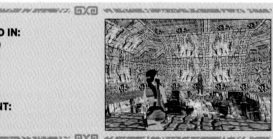

LOCATION FEATURED IN:
Tomb Raider III (1998)

KEY LOCATION:
Caves of Kaliya

MEMORABLE MOMENT:
Defeating Tony

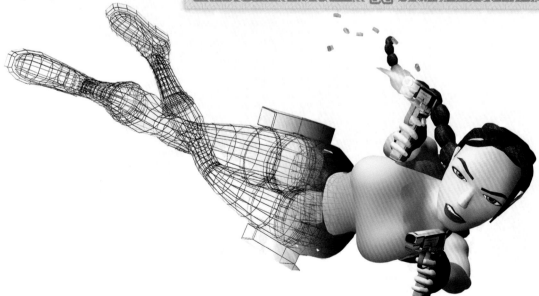

CHINESE CUISINE
TANGHULU

| **LOCATION:** UNDISCLOSED, CHINA | **YIELD:** 12 SKEWERS | **DIFFICULTY RATING:** 1 OUT OF 3 |

Tanghulu is a sweet treat traditionally made from candied Chinese hawberries (or hawthorns) skewered on a bamboo stick, though modern variants using a wider variety of fruits have become commonplace. The fruits are typically emptied out and filled with sweet red bean paste.

RECIPE ORIGINS

Chinese legend suggests that tanghulu was used to save the favorite concubine of Emperor Guangzong of the Song Dynasty. After the emperor's doctors failed to cure her sickness, a common villager suggested eating the candied fruits. To this day, hawberries and their leaves are used in medicine for digestive issues, as well as a wide array of other ailments.

PREP TIME: 10 MINUTES   **COOK TIME:** 20 MINUTES   **INACTIVE TIME:** 10 MINUTES

TOOLS NEEDED: 12 skewers, Small pot, Candy thermometer, Parchment paper

INGREDIENTS:

12 strawberries

2 cups granulated sugar

1 cup water

DIRECTIONS:

1. Wash the strawberries, dry well with a paper towel, and place one on the bottom of each skewer. Set aside.

2. Mix together the sugar and water in a small pot. Bring to a boil, and do not stir the contents. Cook for 8 to 10 minutes, or until the sugar has dissolved and the sugar-water mixture reaches 300°F. (It will become thick and slightly browned.) To test that it's at the right consistency, dip a clean skewer in the pot and then dip that skewer in a glass of cold water. If the sugar hardens, it's ready.

3. Dip the skewered strawberries fully into the sugar mixture, allowing excess sugar to drip off, and then set on parchment paper until it's cooled and hardened (about 10 minutes). Eat immediately.

LOCATION FEATURED IN:
Tomb Raider II (1997)

KEY LOCATION:
The Great Wall

MEMORABLE MOMENTS:
Slaying a dragon

CAMBODIAN CUISINE
LORT CHA

| **LOCATION:** ANGKOR WAT, CAMBODIA | **YIELD:** 2 LARGE SERVINGS | **DIFFICULTY RATING:** 1 OUT OF 3 |

Combined with vegetables and served with a fried egg, Cambodian stir-fry noodles make for a virtually effortless and economical meal. This delicious umami dish is found throughout Cambodia and can be further enhanced with meat and regional condiments such as soy or chili sauce.

RECIPE ORIGINS

Cambodian cuisine has been influenced over the generations by Thailand, Vietnam, France, Spain, and Portugal. The spread of rice noodles and stir-fry techniques, in particular, are traced back to Chinese immigrants beginning during the thirteenth century.

PREP TIME: 15 MINUTES (PLUS 1 HOUR IF MAKING THE RICE PIN NOODLES FROM SCRATCH)   **COOK TIME:** 15 MINUTES

TOOLS NEEDED: Medium bowl, Small bowl, Wok or large pan, Small frying pan

INGREDIENTS:

MEAT:

8 ounces chicken breast, thinly sliced

1 tablespoon oyster sauce

1 tablespoon fish sauce

1 teaspoon cornstarch

STIR FRY:

1 tablespoon dark soy sauce

1 tablespoon oyster sauce

1 tablespoon fish sauce

2 teaspoons granulated sugar

2 tablespoons vegetable oil, divided

4 cloves garlic, minced

8 stalks chives (or green onion, white and green parts separated), cut into 2-inch chunks

2 cups yu choy (or bok choy)

1 pound rice pin noodles*

2 cups bean sprouts, blanched

2 eggs

Chili sauce, to taste

DIRECTIONS:

1. Place the chicken in a bowl and cover with the oyster sauce, fish sauce, and cornstarch. Mix together and let sit for 15 minutes to marinate.

2. To make the stir-fry, mix the soy sauce, oyster sauce, fish sauce, and sugar together in a small bowl. Set aside.

3. Heat a tablespoon of vegetable oil in a wok or large pan over high heat. Add the chicken to the wok and cook undisturbed for 90 seconds, allowing it to sear. Flip to the other side and cook for another 90 seconds, or until the chicken is fully cooked. Place the cooked chicken on a plate to the side.

4. Heat another tablespoon of vegetable oil in the same wok over medium-high heat. Add the garlic and the chives (or the white parts of the green onion), and cook until garlic is browned.

5. Add the yu choy to the pan, and fry for 1 to 2 minutes, or until softened.

6. Add the rice pin noodles, cooked chicken, and the sauce mixture, and cook for 2 to 3 minutes, until everything is evenly covered with the sauce.

7. Add the bean sprouts and green onions, and fry for 1 more minute. Turn off the heat.

8. In a small frying pan, fry the eggs over medium heat. (Cook for 3 minutes, or until the whites are set, then flip and cook for 2 minutes more. The yolk shouldn't be fully set.)

9. Divide the noodles among two plates, and top each plate with a fried egg. Top with a splash of chili sauce, to taste.

*Rice pin noodles, or silver pin noodles, can be found at some specialty Asian markets. If not available near you, you can make them (see following page).

Continued on page 110

Continued from page 109

RICE PIN NOODLES:

1 cup rice flour

1 cup wheat starch

3 tablespoons tapioca starch/tapioca flour

½ teaspoon kosher salt

1 cup boiling water

10. In a large bowl, mix together the rice flour, wheat starch, tapioca starch, and salt. Add the boiling water, and mix with a spatula until it forms a dough.

11. Once cool enough to touch, remove the dough from the bowl and knead on a floured surface for 2 minutes, or until it's nice and smooth.

12. Separate the dough into 10 sections, and roll them out into a long log about ½ inch in diameter. Cut it into ½-inch sections, and taking one section at a time, roll it into a 2-inch-long noodle. Allow the middle to be thicker and the ends to taper. Place the finished noodle on a floured tray.

13. Continue with the rest of the dough.

14. To cook, place in a large pot of boiling water, and cook for 2 to 3 minutes, or until the noodles start to float.

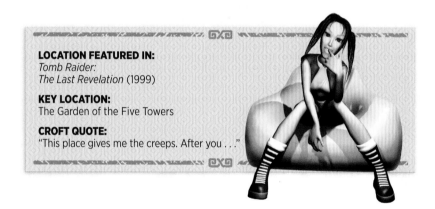

LOCATION FEATURED IN:
Tomb Raider:
The Last Revelation (1999)

KEY LOCATION:
The Garden of the Five Towers

CROFT QUOTE:
"This place gives me the creeps. After you . . ."

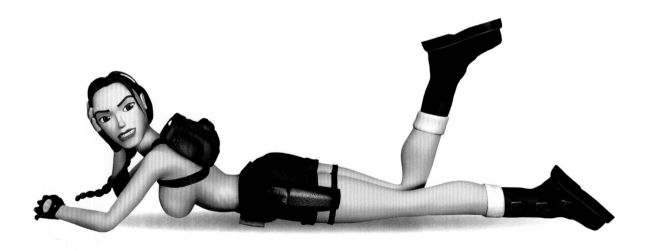

TIBETAN CUISINE
PO CHA

| ◐ **LOCATION:** UNDISCLOSED, TIBET | 🫙 **YIELD:** 4 CUPS OF TEA | 🔥 **DIFFICULTY RATING:** 1 OUT OF 3 |

Po cha, sometimes referred to as butter tea, is a popular drink throughout the Himalayas. Tea leaves are traditionally combined with yak or cow butter, water, and salt for a warm and filling tea sometimes necessary for survival in the areas from which it originates. Yak butter is expensive and difficult to come by in the colder seasons, so butter tea may be reserved for guests and special occasions. Like many types of tea, po cha is often personalized to taste; some people keep it simple and skip the half-and-half. Others add star anise, a regional flower pod that gives a sweet, licorice-like flavor. And while butter tea is intended to be salty, some directly add sugar to taste.

RECIPE ORIGINS

Tea is believed to have made its way to Tibet with Chinese Princess Wencheng, who married Tibetan King Songtsen Gampo around 634 CE. Combining tea with the most common form of butter available in Tibet was a natural decision, as it provided warmth, energy, and sustenance needed to survive in the frigid climate.

🕐 **COOK TIME:** 5 MINUTES

TOOLS NEEDED: Kettle or pot for boiling water, Blender

INGREDIENTS:

4 cups water

2 tablespoons black tea (or 2 teabags)

2 tablespoons unsalted butter

½ cup half-and-half

½ teaspoon kosher salt

DIRECTIONS:

1. Boil the water, and steep the tea for 3 to 5 minutes (the longer you steep, the more caffeinated the tea will be).

2. Add the butter to the tea, and stir gently until melted. Pour that mixture, half-and-half, and salt into a blender, and blend on high for 60 seconds, or until frothy.

3. Pour into 4 separate cups and serve.

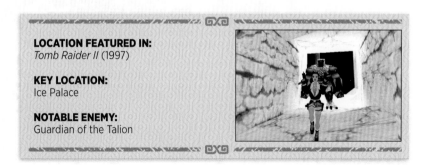

LOCATION FEATURED IN:
Tomb Raider II (1997)

KEY LOCATION:
Ice Palace

NOTABLE ENEMY:
Guardian of the Talion

JAPANESE CUISINE
OKONOMIYAKI

LOCATION: TOKYO, JAPAN | **YIELD:** 2 PANCAKES | **DIFFICULTY RATING:** 2 OUT OF 3

Okonomiyaki are savory Japanese pancakes typically embellished with extravagant toppings. Preparation varies between regions, and many restaurants serve raw okonomiyaki ingredients as part of a cook-it-yourself experience. Unlike sweet pancakes, this hearty dish typically contains cabbage, yam, vegetables, and meat such as bacon, pork, or octopus, and is topped with pickled ginger, seaweed flakes, or Japanese mayonnaise. Okonomiyaki is derived from the word "okonomi," meaning "how you like." There are countless variations to this recipe, but this Osaka-style version is one of the more popular ways you'll see it offered in Tokyo.

RECIPE ORIGINS

According to the *Heibonsha World Encyclopedia*, modern okonomiyaki originates from crêpes that became popular after the 1923 Great Kanto earthquake. The crêpes were made using the limited supplies available at the time. The recipes evolved and expanded over time to include savory variants and were favored as a filling and inexpensive snack for children during World War II.

PREP TIME: 5 MINUTES   **COOK TIME:** 30 MINUTES

TOOLS NEEDED: Large mixing bowl, Large skillet with a lid, Spatula

INGREDIENTS:

SAUCE:
2 tablespoons ketchup

2 tablespoons Worcestershire sauce

1 tablespoon soy sauce

1 tablespoon oyster sauce

1 tablespoon granulated sugar

PANCAKE:
1 cup all-purpose flour

¼ teaspoon kosher salt

¼ teaspoon granulated sugar

¼ teaspoon baking powder

¾ cup dashi stock

2 eggs

4 cups of cabbage, sliced into thin strips no longer than 3 inches each

4 green onions, sliced thin

2 tablespoons minced pickled red ginger

2 tablespoons vegetable oil, divided

½ pound sliced pork belly or bacon

TOPPINGS:
Japanese mayonnaise

Dried bonito flakes

Dried seaweed

Chopped green onions

LOCATION FEATURED IN:
Tomb Raider: Legend (2006)

KEY LOCATION:
Takamoto's party

MEMORABLE MOMENTS:
Jumping across buildings on a motorbike

Continued on page 114

Continued from page 113

DIRECTIONS:

1. To make the okonomiyaki sauce: Combine the ketchup, Worcestershire sauce, soy sauce, oyster sauce, and sugar in a small bowl. Set aside.

2. To make the batter: Mix together the flour, salt, sugar, and baking powder in a large bowl. Add the dashi stock and eggs, and mix.

3. Add the cabbage, green onions, and pickled red ginger to the bowl, mixing until the cabbage is fully coated.

4. Heat 1 tablespoon of vegetable oil on medium heat in a large skillet. Spoon half of the okonomiyaki batter into the skillet in a 1-inch-thick "pancake" about 8 inches in diameter. Lay half of the pork belly or bacon slices on top of the okonomiyaki. Cover the skillet, and let cook for 5 minutes, or until the bottom has browned.

5. Carefully flip it so the pork is now on the bottom, increase the heat to medium-high, and let it cook for 5 to 7 minutes, or until the pork is brown and sizzling and the inside of the "pancake" appears to be cooked through.

6. Place the okonomiyaki on a plate. Brush 1 heaping tablespoon of the okonomiyaki sauce all over the top, and then squeeze Japanese mayonnaise over the top in a thin zigzag pattern. Top with sprinklings of bonito flakes, seaweed, and green onion.

7. Repeat steps 4–7 for the second pancake.

JAPANESE CUISINE
SEAWEED SALAD

| **LOCATION:** YAMATAI, JAPAN | **YIELD:** 4 SMALL SERVINGS | **DIFFICULTY RATING:** 1 OUT OF 3 |

Wakame is a subtly sweet edible seaweed most commonly served in Japanese salads and miso soup. Goma wakame, or seaweed salad, is popular among Western sushi restaurants and includes sesame seeds as a key ingredient. Wakame is high in healthy nutrients such as omega-3 fatty acids, but also notably high in sodium and should be consumed in moderation.

RECIPE ORIGINS

Japanese sea-farmers have harvested and grown wakame since at least the Nara period (710–794 CE). Japan, Korea, and China are the three largest consumers of edible seaweed, harvesting an estimated 6 million tons each year. Native to Japan, wakame has been listed by the International Union for Conservation of Nature as one of the world's one hundred most invasive species, particularly in countries such as New Zealand, Europe, Australia, and the United States.

PREP TIME: 10 MINUTES   **COOK TIME:** 5 MINUTES

TOOLS NEEDED: 3 medium bowls

INGREDIENTS:

1 ounce dried seaweed (wakame or a variety)

2 tablespoons rice vinegar

1 tablespoon soy sauce

1 tablespoon sesame oil

2 teaspoons granulated sugar

½ teaspoon minced garlic

¼ teaspoon grated ginger

2 green onions, thinly sliced

1 tablespoon toasted sesame seeds

DIRECTIONS:

1. Rehydrate the seaweed by placing it in a bowl of water for 10 minutes.

2. While the seaweed is rehydrating, make the dressing. In a medium bowl, whisk together the rice vinegar, soy sauce, sesame oil, sugar, garlic, and ginger until the sugar is dissolved and the ingredients are fully combined.

3. Drain the seaweed and gently squeeze out any excess water. If the seaweed pieces are large, cut them into ½-inch-wide strips.

4. Place the seaweed and green onions in a bowl, and top with the dressing. Mix until it's all evenly dressed.

5. Divide evenly between 4 small plates and top with sesame seeds.

LOCATION FEATURED IN:
Tomb Raider (2013)

KEY LOCATION:
Shipwreck Beach

CROFT QUOTE:
"A famous explorer once said that the extraordinary is in what we do, not who we are."

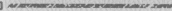

MOMOS

| **LOCATION:** UNDISCLOSED, NEPAL | **YIELD:** 50 MOMOS (AROUND 5 SERVINGS) | **DIFFICULTY RATING:** 3 OUT OF 3 |

Native to Nepal, momos are steamed dumplings filled with pork, chicken, buffalo, or goat meat. Cheese or vegetable variants also exist, as do regional differences where other types of meats may be more readily available than those found in Nepal. The dish has become a traditional delicacy in Nepal and the surrounding nations. Although not a traditional cooking method, those without a steamer can cook these with a large pan and lid.

RECIPE ORIGINS

Momos date back to the early Newar people, the founders of the Kingdom of Nepal (1768). Although the Newari comprise only 5 percent of the modern-day Nepal population, their traditions and cuisine are observed throughout the country.

PREP TIME: 2 HOURS

COOK TIME: 20 MINUTES

TOOLS NEEDED: 2 large bowls, Steamer, Nonstick pan, Blender

INGREDIENTS:

WRAPPER:

4 cups all-purpose flour

1½ cups room-temperature water

1 tablespoon vegetable oil

1 pinch of salt

FILLING:

1 pound ground chicken

1 pound ground pork

½ cup chopped cilantro

1 cup diced red onion

½ cup diced green onion

3 tablespoons salted butter, melted

2 tablespoons minced garlic

2 tablespoons minced ginger

2 tablespoons cumin

1 tablespoon curry powder

1 teaspoon cinnamon

1 pinch of salt

1 pinch of black pepper

TOMATO ACHAR:

1 tablespoon vegetable oil

4 plum tomatoes, quartered

½ yellow onion, diced

2 dried red chilies

1 tablespoon minced garlic

½ tablespoon minced ginger

1 tablespoon cumin

2 teaspoons turmeric

Salt, to taste

2 tablespoons cilantro, chopped

LOCATION FEATURED IN:
Tomb Raider: Legend (2006)

KEY LOCATION:
Airplane Crash Site

CROFT QUOTE:
"Once again I am compelled to go into my own past."

Continued on page 118

Continued from page 117

DIRECTIONS:

1. To make the wrappers, mix the flour, water, vegetable oil, and salt in a large bowl. Mix and knead it in the bowl for 10 minutes, or until it creates a soft, firm, stretchy dough. Cover the bowl with plastic wrap, and let rest for 30 minutes.

2. Meanwhile, make the filling by mixing ground chicken, ground pork, cilantro, red onion, green onion, garlic, ginger, cumin, curry powder, cinnamon, salt, and pepper in a large bowl, cover with plastic wrap, and refrigerate until needed.

3. To make the tomato achar, heat the oil in a nonstick pan over medium heat, then add tomatoes, onion, chilies, garlic, ginger, cumin, turmeric, and salt. Cook for 10 minutes, or until the liquid in the tomatoes has reduced. Remove from heat and stir in the cilantro. Carefully pour the mixture into a blender, and blend until smooth. If you don't have a blender, you can leave it chunky. Refrigerate until ready to use.

4. Take the dough, and separate it into approximately 50 1-inch balls. Work with a few pieces of dough at a time, keeping the rest in the bowl covered in plastic wrap.

5. Using your palm, flatten the balls into discs, and then use a rolling pin to roll the discs into thin circles, 3 inches in diameter. The edges should be thinner than the middle.

6. Remove the filling from the refrigerator. Place 1 tablespoon of filling in the middle of each circle, then close it in a pouch/moneybag style: pinch part of the edge of the wrapper, slowly adding in another section of the edge, pinching and pleating your way around until it's all gathered up in the center of the momo. Give a final twist and pinch in the middle to close it fully.

7. Repeat steps 5 and 6 for the rest of the momos.

8. Oil your steamer and heat it up. Place the momos inside, and steam for 10 minutes, or until fully cooked through. (To test, take one out and cut it open to confirm the meat is fully cooked.) If you don't have a steamer, heat 2 tablespoons of oil in a large pan over medium-high heat. Place the momos in the pan and cover the bottom of the pan in a small layer of water. Cover, reduce heat to medium, and let cook for 10 minutes, or until fully cooked through.

9. Continue steaming the rest of the momos, and serve with tomato achar.

KAZAKHSTANI CUISINE
BAURSAK

LOCATION: UNDISCLOSED, KAZAKHSTAN | **YIELD:** 30 PIECES OF FRIED DOUGH | **DIFFICULTY RATING:** 2 OUT OF 3

Kazakh baursak is a fried dough typically shaped as a triangle or sphere and served as an appetizer or dessert. It is a cousin of the traditional doughnut, though is more akin to a cookie or biscuit based on the preparation.

RECIPE ORIGINS

Baursak originates from Mongolia, where it is known as "boortsog" and traditionally made with mutton fat rather than vegetable oil, and served with tea.

PREP TIME: 15 MINUTES   **COOK TIME:** 35 MINUTES   **INACTIVE TIME:** 2 HOURS

TOOLS NEEDED: Small bowl, Stand mixer, Large heavy-bottomed pot or Dutch oven, Kitchen thermometer, Slotted spoon

INGREDIENTS:

¼ cup milk, lukewarm

1 tablespoon active dry yeast

1 tablespoon unsalted butter

½ tablespoon granulated sugar

1 egg

¼ cup water

¼ teaspoon kosher salt

2 cups all-purpose flour

Vegetable oil, for frying

Powdered sugar, for garnish

DIRECTIONS:

1. Mix the lukewarm milk and the yeast together in a small bowl. Let sit 10 minutes, or until the yeast is frothy.

2. In a medium mixing bowl, mix together the butter and sugar until they're fully incorporated. Add the egg, and mix.

3. Add the milk mixture, water, salt, and half of the flour. Mix on low just until combined. Add the rest of the flour slowly, mixing until combined.

4. Cover the bowl with a moist towel and let rest somewhere warm for 2 hours, or until the dough doubles in size.

5. Place the dough on a floured surface, and roll out to a large rectangle ¼-inch thick.

6. Cut the dough into 2-inch-wide strips, and then cut the other direction, making 2-inch dough squares.

7. Heat 2 inches' worth of vegetable oil in a large pot or Dutch oven to 350°F.

8. Working in batches to avoid overcrowding, place the rectangles in the hot oil, frying for 1 minute on each side. Remove with a slotted spoon and place on a paper towel–lined plate to drain any excess oil.

9. Sift powdered sugar over the donuts and enjoy.

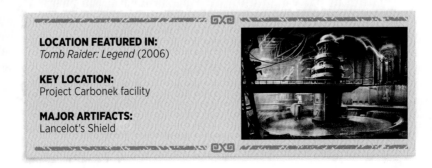

LOCATION FEATURED IN:
Tomb Raider: Legend (2006)

KEY LOCATION:
Project Carbonek facility

MAJOR ARTIFACTS:
Lancelot's Shield

ANDAMAN CUISINE
COCONUT PRAWN CURRY

| **◐ LOCATION:** ANDAMAN SEA | **🥫 YIELD:** 4 SERVINGS | **🔥 DIFFICULTY RATING:** 1 OUT OF 3 |

For a swift and flavorful dish, coconut prawn curry is a guaranteed crowd-pleaser. Combine marinated prawns, stir-fry, and aromatic curry to form a creamy amalgamation of amazing flavors and textures.

RECIPE ORIGINS

Curry originated in India as early as 2600 BCE and spread throughout Asia along ancient trade routes. Leaves from curry trees are not a required component outside of India, while turmeric is the essential spice that provides curry with its distinct taste.

⏱ PREP TIME: 5 MINUTES   **⏱ COOK TIME:** 15 MINUTES

TOOLS NEEDED: Large pan or wok

INGREDIENTS:

1 tablespoon coconut oil

½ yellow onion, thinly sliced

1 red bell pepper, thinly sliced

3 cloves garlic, minced

1 tablespoon grated ginger

¼ cup red curry paste

1 (14.5 oz) can full-fat coconut milk

1 tablespoon light brown sugar, packed

1 tablespoon fish sauce

1 pound prawns, peeled, cleaned, and heads removed (or large shrimp, peeled and deveined)

1½ cups snow peas

Juice and zest of 1 small lime

2 tablespoons chopped cilantro

4 cups jasmine rice, cooked

Thai basil, for serving

DIRECTIONS:

1. Heat oil in a large nonstick pan or wok over medium-high heat. Add onion, bell pepper, garlic, ginger, and curry paste to the pan, and sauté for 3 minutes, or until the onions are softened and the mixture is fragrant.

2. Add the coconut milk, brown sugar, and fish sauce. Bring to a boil, and then simmer for 3 minutes.

3. Add the prawns and snow peas, and cook for 7 to 8 minutes, or until the prawns are opaque and fully cooked through.

4. Mix in the lime zest and juice and a sprinkling of cilantro.

5. Serve with jasmine rice and top with Thai basil leaves.

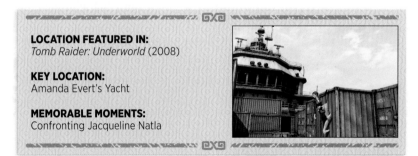

LOCATION FEATURED IN:
Tomb Raider: Underworld (2008)

KEY LOCATION:
Amanda Evert's Yacht

MEMORABLE MOMENTS:
Confronting Jacqueline Natla

THAI CUISINE
MANGO STICKY RICE

| ◁ **LOCATION:** UNDISCLOSED, COASTAL THAILAND | ⬚ **YIELD:** 6 SERVINGS | ⚲ **DIFFICULTY RATING:** 1 OUT OF 3 |

A sweet and straightforward traditional Thai dessert, mango sticky rice is typically a seasonal dish sold during peak mango season, which varies from country to country. While this recipe uses the traditional method of steaming the rice, you're welcome to use a rice cooker as a more modern alternative.

RECIPE ORIGINS

Rice is a fundamental staple of Thai cuisine. Thai folklore involves the worshipping of the rice goddess, Mae Phosop. Queen Sirkit renewed this practice in 2008, and the ancient custom is linked to the annual plowing ceremonies that mark the beginning of the rice-plowing season.

◷ **PREP TIME:** 10 MINUTES   ◷ **COOK TIME:** 25 MINUTES   ◷ **INACTIVE TIME:** 2 HOURS AND 30 MINUTES

TOOLS NEEDED: Small bowl, Sieve, Large saucepan or steamer, Small saucepan

INGREDIENTS:

1½ cups sweet (glutinous) rice

1⅓ cups canned unsweetened coconut milk

½ cup granulated sugar

¼ teaspoon kosher salt

Sesame seeds, for topping

2 large ripe mangos, peeled, pitted, and cut into 18 thin slices

DIRECTIONS:

1. Rinse rice in a bowl multiple times, until the water runs clear. Cover the rice with cold water, and let it soak for at least 2 hours.

2. Drain the rice in a sieve, and put the sieve over a large pot filled with a couple of inches of simmering water. Cover the pot, and steam for 25 to 30 minutes, or until the rice is cooked, turning the rice over once at the halfway point. (If you have a steamer basket, you can use that instead of the sieve—just put a cheesecloth over the steamer basket to make sure the rice won't fall through the holes.)

3. While the rice cooks, bring the coconut milk, sugar, and salt to a simmer in a small saucepan, and cook for 1 to 2 minutes, or until the sugar is fully dissolved. Set aside.

4. Mix together the cooked rice and 1½ cups of the coconut milk mixture in a small bowl. Cover and let stand for 30 minutes, or until the coconut milk mixture is fully absorbed. Refrigerate the rest of the coconut milk mixture (you'll use this as a sauce when plating).

5. To plate, place a large ice cream scoop of sticky rice on a plate. Drizzle with the coconut milk sauce, and top with a sprinkle of sesame seeds. Place 3 slices of mango on top of the rice.

LOCATION FEATURED IN:
Tomb Raider: Underworld (2008)

KEY LOCATION:
The Lost City of Bhogavati

NOTABLE ENEMIES:
Naga

SYRIAN CUISINE
MANA'EESH

| ⟨⟩ **LOCATION:** UNDISCLOSED, SYRIA | ▯ **YIELD:** 4 MANA'EESH | ⚶ **DIFFICULTY RATING:** 2 OUT OF 3 |

Mana'eesh is a savory pastry popular in the Levant (Eastern Mediterranean). Mana'eesh is most commonly topped with za'atar and olive oil and served with garden vegetables. Feta cheese or labneh (yogurt cheese) complements the earthy flavor of the spices.

RECIPE ORIGINS

Written recordings dating back to the tenth century make note of mana'eesh-style meals. It was made from leftover dough used during morning baking—a practice still common to this day.

⏱ **PREP TIME:** 10 MINUTES ⏱ **COOK TIME:** 25 MINUTES ⏱ **INACTIVE TIME:** 90 MINUTES

TOOLS NEEDED: Kitchen towel, Pizza stone or parchment paper–lined baking sheet

INGREDIENTS:

DOUGH:

1 packet (2¼ teaspoons) active dry yeast

1 teaspoon granulated sugar

1 cup lukewarm water

3 cups all-purpose flour

1 teaspoon kosher salt

2 tablespoons olive oil

TOPPING:

¼ cup za'atar*

¼ cup olive oil

LOCATION FEATURED IN:
Rise of the Tomb Raider (2015)

KEY LOCATION:
The Prophet's Tomb

MEMORABLE MOMENTS:
Escaping the collapsing tomb

DIRECTIONS:

1. Mix the yeast, sugar, and water in a small bowl. Let sit for 10 minutes, or until the yeast has started to look foamy.

2. In a large bowl, mix the flour and salt together. Make a well in the middle of the mixture, and add the olive oil and yeast water.

3. Mix together with your hands until it starts to form a ball, then remove from the bowl and knead for 5 minutes on a floured surface. You'll know you're done kneading when you poke the dough and it springs back.

4. Place the dough ball back into the large bowl, and cover with a damp towel. Let rise in a warm spot until it doubles in size, 1 to 2 hours.

5. Place the dough back on the floured surface, and divide into 4 smaller balls. Cover with the towel and let rise for 30 additional minutes.

6. Place a floured pizza stone or a parchment paper–lined baking sheet in the oven, and preheat it to 400°F.

7. Roll out the dough balls into discs about 8 inches in diameter and ¼-inch thick.

8. Mix together the za'atar and olive oil in a small bowl. Place a heaping tablespoon of the za'atar mixture in the middle of each disc and spread it evenly with the back of a spoon, leaving a bare "crust" along the edge. Use a floured pizza peel (or your hands) to move it onto the pizza stone or baking sheet in the oven.

9. Bake for 7 to 10 minutes, or until the mana'eesh is browned on the edges.

10. Let cool for a few minutes and enjoy while warm.

---

*Can't find za'atar? Make your own by mixing together 1 tablespoon each of sumac, dried oregano, and toasted sesame seeds; ½ tablespoon each of dried thyme and marjoram; and 1 teaspoon kosher salt.

PELMENI

| ⟨ LOCATION: SIBERIA, RUSSIA **|** 🗑 **YIELD:** ABOUT 100 PELMENI (5 SERVINGS) **|** 🔥 **DIFFICULTY RATING:** 2 OUT OF 3

Pelmeni are Russian dumplings typically served with butter and sour cream. Although quite popular and perfect for the cold Russian climate, quite a bit of work is required to make a serving of pelmeni. Thankfully, they can be made in large batches and served across several meals, with store-bought options for those short on time.

RECIPE ORIGINS

The debate around the origins of pelmeni are ongoing. Siberia is famous for its pelmeni, but the word "pelmeni" itself is derived from the Udmurt word "pelnyan," or "ear bread," an obvious reference to the dumpling's appearance and ingredients. Indeed, pelmeni was exclusive to Siberian and Ural cuisine until the mid-nineteenth century.

🕐 **PREP TIME:** 10 MINUTES   🕐 **COOK TIME:** 45 MINUTES   🕐 **INACTIVE TIME:** 90 MINUTES

TOOLS NEEDED: 2 large bowls, Shot glass or 1½-inch cookie cutter, Rimmed baking sheet

INGREDIENTS:

DOUGH:

3 cups all-purpose flour

1 teaspoon kosher salt

2 eggs, beaten

¾ cup water

FILLING:

¼ pound ground beef

¼ pound ground pork

½ yellow onion, diced

2 cloves garlic, minced

1 tablespoon vegetable oil

½ teaspoon kosher salt

½ teaspoon black pepper

TOPPING:

Butter, optional

Sour Cream, optional

LOCATION FEATURED IN:
Rise of the Tomb Raider (2015)

KEY LOCATION:
Geothermal Valley

ESSENTIAL EQUIPMENT:
Bow and Arrow

DIRECTIONS:

1. Place the flour in a mound on a cutting board or other work surface. Make a well in the middle, and add the salt, eggs, and water. Slowly work the flour into the middle, and combine until it forms a dough. Knead for 5 minutes, or until the dough is firm and no longer sticky.

2. Place the dough in a large bowl, and cover with plastic wrap. Refrigerate for 30 minutes.

3. Right before bringing the dough back out, mix the ground beef, ground pork, onion, garlic, oil, salt, and pepper in a large bowl. Set aside.

4. Break the dough into two pieces, and keep one in the bowl. Roll the other one out on a floured surface to about ⅛-inch thick. Using the rim of a shot glass or a small cookie cutter, cut the dough into circles approximately 1½ inches in diameter.

5. Place ½ teaspoon of filling onto one half of each circle, and fold the dough over into a half-moon shape. Pinch the edges closed, and then bring up the two ends to meet, completing a circle. Pinch together.

6. Continue until all the dough and filling are gone.

7. Place the pelmeni onto a parchment paper–covered rimmed baking pan, and place in the freezer for 1 hour. After that, you can cook them, or move them to a freezer-safe bag for longer storage.

8. When ready to cook them, place the pelmeni in a large pot of boiling water and cook for 5 minutes, or until they float to the top.

9. Serve with melted butter or sour cream.

RUSSIAN CUISINE
PIROZHKI

| ☾ **LOCATION:** BARENTS SEA, RUSSIA | 🏺 **YIELD:** 8 PIROZHKI | 🔥 **DIFFICULTY RATING:** 2 OUT OF 3 |

A pirozhok is a typically boat-shaped bun with an enclosed filling. It can be baked or fried, large or small, and popular fillings include meat, mashed potatoes, cabbage, fruit, and jam. Pirozhki are wildly popular comfort foods in Russia.

🕐 **PREP TIME:** 15 MINUTES   🕐 **COOK TIME:** 45 MINUTES   🕐 **INACTIVE TIME:** 1 HOUR

TOOLS NEEDED: 1 small bowl, 1 stand mixer, 1 large pot, 1 large bowl, Dutch oven or heavy-bottomed pot, Kitchen thermometer

INGREDIENTS:

DOUGH:

1 (2¼ teaspoons) package active dry yeast

1 tablespoon granulated sugar

1½ cups warm milk, divided

2 tablespoons unsalted butter, melted

1 egg

1½ teaspoons kosher salt

4 cups all-purpose flour, divided

Vegetable oil, for frying

FILLING:

4 russet potatoes (about 2 pounds), peeled and cut into 1-inch chunks

3 tablespoons salted butter

1 tablespoon fresh dill, minced

2 tablespoons vegetable oil

2 medium or 1 large yellow onion, diced

Salt and black pepper, to taste

LOCATION FEATURED IN:
Tomb Raider: Chronicles (2000)

KEY LOCATION:
Russian Submarine

ESSENTIAL EQUIPMENT:
Extreme-Depth Suit

DIRECTIONS:

1. Combine the yeast, sugar, and ½ cup warm milk in a small bowl. Let stand 10 minutes, or until foamy.

2. In a separate mixing bowl, add the rest of the warm milk, butter, egg, salt, and 1 cup of flour. Mix with a dough hook on low until just combined. Add the yeast mixture, and mix. Add the rest of the flour, one cup at a time, and mix until the dough is fully mixed and elastic. If you don't have a mixer, mix the ingredients with a spatula and then knead on a floured surface until the dough becomes elastic.

3. Cover the bowl with a damp towel, and let rise until doubled in size, at least 1 hour.

4. While that's rising, prepare the filling. Bring a large pot of salted water to boil, and boil the potatoes for 10 to 12 minutes or until they can be easily pierced by a fork. Drain and mash the potatoes in a large bowl. Mix in the butter and dill.

5. Heat the vegetable oil in a pan over medium heat, and add the onions. Sauté for 5 minutes, or until the onions are soft, translucent, and getting brown.

6. Add the sautéed onions to the potato mixture. Mix, and add salt and pepper to taste.

7. Remove the risen dough from its bowl and place on a floured surface. Cut the dough into 8 equal sections, roll into a ball, and then roll out into a 6-inch circle, approximately ⅛-inch thick.

8. In each circle, put ½ cup filling in the center of the bottom half of the circle. Then close the other half of the circle over the top. Pinch the edges together to fully seal the pirozhok.

9. Preheat a Dutch oven or heavy-bottomed pot with 3 inches of vegetable oil to 375°F.

10. Using a flat spatula, carefully lower the pirozhki into the oil, only cooking a couple at a time to reduce crowding. Cook on one side for 2 minutes, then flip and cook for 1 minute on the other side. Remove from the pot and let drain on a paper towel–lined plate.

11. Serve warm with sour cream.

AUSTRALIAN CUISINE
ANZAC BISCUITS

| **LOCATION:** UNDISCLOSED, AUSTRALIA | **YIELD:** 18 TO 24 COOKIES | **DIFFICULTY RATING:** 1 OUT OF 3 |

This sweet biscuit made from rolled oats and syrup is popular in Australia and New Zealand. "Anzac" is a legally protected term and cannot be used commercially without permission from the Minister of Veterans' Affairs. Primary enforcement around Anzac biscuits includes ensuring production stays true to the original recipe and that the treat is never referred to as a "cookie." While the traditional recipe wouldn't have included coconut, more modern recipes use the ingredient, which adds a delicious flavor.

RECIPE ORIGINS

The Anzac biscuit's name is derived from the Australian and New Zealand Army Corps (ANZAC), which was established during World War I. Variations of what would eventually become the modern-day recipe first appeared throughout the 1910s in Australian and New Zealand cookbooks. Because of the historical tie to the ANZAC, Anzac biscuits are manufactured and sold as part of fundraising efforts for the modern Australian and New Zealand military forces. Rumor has it that Australian and New Zealand women sent these biscuits to soldiers during World War I because they don't spoil easily and can keep well while traveling.

PREP TIME: 5 MINUTES   **COOK TIME:** 25 MINUTES

TOOLS NEEDED: Large bowl, Small saucepan, Parchment paper–covered baking sheet, Wire rack

INGREDIENTS:

1 cup all-purpose flour

1 cup rolled oats

¾ cup shredded coconut

½ cup light brown sugar, packed

¼ cup granulated sugar

8 tablespoons (½ cup) salted butter

2 tablespoons golden syrup
(or 1 tablespoon corn syrup and
1 tablespoon honey)

2 tablespoons water

1 teaspoon baking soda

DIRECTIONS:

1. Preheat the oven to 325°F.

2. Mix the flour, oats, coconut, brown sugar, and granulated sugar together in a large bowl.

3. Heat the butter, syrup, and water together in a small saucepan over medium-low heat until the butter melts. Remove from heat and add the baking soda. Add the warm syrup mixture to the dry mixture in the bowl, and combine.

4. Roll a heaping ½ tablespoon of mixture into a small ball, and place on a parchment paper–covered baking sheet. Repeat with the rest of the dough, leaving 1 inch between each ball for spreading.

5. Bake for 12 minutes, or until golden brown. Remove from the oven and let firm up on the baking sheet for 2 minutes, then move to a wire rack to cool completely.

LOCATION FEATURED IN:
Tomb Raider: The Series Vol. 1,
Issue 42 (2004)

KEY LOCATION:
Sydney

MAJOR ARTIFACT:
The Spirit Walker

POLYNESIAN CUISINE
'OTAI

| ◖ **LOCATION:** UNDISCLOSED, SOUTH PACIFIC | ▮ **YIELD:** 2 LITERS (4 SERVINGS) | ♦ **DIFFICULTY RATING:** 1 OUT OF 3

'Otai is a Western Polynesian fruit drink served as a refreshment during summer gatherings. Common fruit ingredients include watermelon, pineapple, and coconut, and are to be shredded rather than blended.

RECIPE ORIGINS

'Otai is generally attributed to the Kingdom of Tonga, a Polynesian country comprised of 169 islands. The ingredients used to make 'Otai are plentiful throughout the Tonga archipelago and the surrounding countries, such as Fiji and Samoa, where similar drinks are common.

COOK TIME: 10 MINUTES

INACTIVE TIME: 30 MINUTES

TOOLS NEEDED: Blender, Pitcher

INGREDIENTS:

1 (20-ounce) can crushed pineapple in juice

1 (13.5-ounce) can coconut milk

1 cup coconut water

Juice from 1 lime

Seedless watermelon (about 6 cups' worth)

DIRECTIONS:

1. Blend the crushed pineapple and juice, coconut milk, coconut water, and lime juice until smooth.

2. Scoop the watermelon out into a large bowl and grate it, mash it, or shred it with forks until it's in small chunks.

3. Combine the blended contents, the watermelon, and the watermelon juice into a large pitcher and mix together.

4. Chill 30 minutes or until cold, then serve.

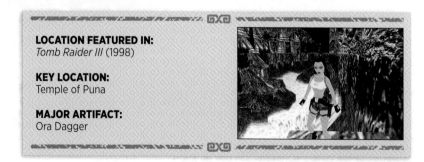

LOCATION FEATURED IN:
Tomb Raider III (1998)

KEY LOCATION:
Temple of Puna

MAJOR ARTIFACT:
Ora Dagger

CHAPTER FIVE
AFRICA

◈ **KEY LOCATIONS:** Khamoon and Varying Locations, Egypt; Undisclosed, Ghana

Key Terminology:

- **North Africa:** A geographic and ethno-cultural term that usually includes countries with ties to the Middle East or West Asia, such as Algeria, Egypt, Libya, Morocco, Tunisia, and Sudan.
- **Sub-Saharan Africa:** A term for the region of the African continent south of the Sahara Desert, which boasts a tropical climate.
- **Horn of Africa:** The peninsula jutting out in east Africa which is home to Djibouti, Eritrea, Ethiopia, and Somalia.
- **Congo Basin:** A biodiverse area and important tropical rainforest in central Africa fueled by the Congo River, often just referred to as the Congo.

Africa is believed to be the birthplace of humanity, with early human fossils dating back as far as seven million years. Our ancestors evolved and migrated across Africa and eventually the rest of the world, leaving a wake of emerging civilizations behind them. This makes Africa one of the most important regions in the world to paleoanthropologists for the purposes of understanding the origins of humanity.

Africa is also the second-largest continent and the only continent stretching across the equator from the Northern Hemisphere to the Southern Hemisphere, creating a stunning amount of biodiversity. The Sahara—known also as the Greatest Desert—is the largest hot desert in the world at 3.6 million square miles. It is second only to the cold deserts of Antarctica and the Arctic. It covers the majority of North Africa and alternates between desert and savanna grassland every twenty thousand years, with the next green cycle expected in roughly fifteen millennia.

The Sahara can be accessed through several countries. Morocco offers a centralized airport in Marrakesh with many short and affordable flights from Europe. This will let you travel through the capital city filled with amazing landmarks, museums, and culture, before heading into the Saharan desert with one of many tour options to see oceans of sand, mountains, and hidden oases. The weather is mildest during spring and autumn but can otherwise bounce between impossibly scorching days and frigid nights.

In sharp contrast to the desert region of the Sahara, the Congo Basin, which dominates the Central African region, is the world's second-largest tropic rainforest. Whether it's cruising along the Congo River or adventuring deep in the forest, travel to the Congo is becoming more accessible due to increased infrastructure in the surrounding countries. The Nouabalé-Ndoki National Park in the northern Democratic Republic of Congo is a virtually untouched lowland rainforest offering rare views at some of Africa's most prestigious native wildlife.

Africa as a whole is home to the world's largest megafauna, such as elephants, hippos, giraffes, and rhinoceroses. These animals, along with wild leopards, buffalo, and many more, can be seen from Kruger National Park, a few hours' drive from the South African city of Johannesburg. The park can be explored in guided vehicles, on foot, or via hot-air balloon.

In addition to the well-known Egyptian kingdoms in the north, pre-colonial Africa is believed to have thousands of uniquely identifying groups, from small family-centric clans to large kingdoms that gained wealth from trade routes.

As with other continents, Africa has a history of colonization, famously including the Greek conquest of Egypt. In particular, the late nineteenth and early twentieth centuries are sometimes known as the Scramble for Africa or New Imperialism. At its height, 90 percent of Africa was under European control. Many African countries remained so until a move for independence grew after the conclusion of World War II.

Dismantling European influence is an ongoing pursuit and took longer in some places than others. South Africa was subject to institutionalized racial segregation called apartheid until the 1990s. The effects are still felt throughout South Africa today, including major cities such as Johannesburg, Port Elizabeth, and Cape Town.

Now home to fifty-four unique countries, Africa boasts the youngest population in the world and is an increasingly important economic market. As the world becomes more connected, the varied art and traditions of these diverse African countries are finally being recognized worldwide.

No archeologist's passport would be complete without a trip to Egypt. Arguably putting the "tomb" in Tomb Raider, the mysteries of the pyramids have played no small part in Lara's many adventures, including the original *Tomb Raider* (1996), *Tomb Raider: The Last Revelation* (1999), and *Lara Croft and the Temple of Osiris* (2014), where she fought alongside the Egyptian gods Isis and Horus.

KHAMOON, EGYPT

Khamoon is a fictitious ancient city featured in the original *Tomb Raider* (1996) and was heavily inspired by real-world Egyptian ruins. The City of Khamoon features a statue not dissimilar to the Great Sphinx of Giza just south of Cairo. The mythical creature has a storied past in many cultures. In Greece, there is a singular sphinx associated with an ancient riddle needed to enter the city of Thebes. In Egypt, the sphinx is usually depicted wearing a pharaoh's headdress and placed near tombs or temples as a guardian.

The Sphynx of Giza overlooks three pyramids: the Great Pyramid of Khufu, the Pyramid of Khafre, and the Pyramid of Menkaure. Combined, these grand landmarks are the ones most associated with Egypt and the only one of the Seven Wonders of the Ancient World that remains intact enough to visit. Tours to the pyramids typically depart from Giza or Cairo and may include a cruise along the Nile River, though taxis can also be taken along Pyramids Road. While it is illegal to climb the pyramids themselves, an additional fee will grant you access to their interiors. For the Great Pyramid, you climb through a narrow vertical shaft to get to the King's Chamber, which houses an empty sarcophagus. The visit inside is well worth it for a better understanding of the construction and use of the great structure.

Measuring 240 feet long and standing over 65 feet tall, the Sphynx is the oldest known monumental sculpture in Egypt, carved from a single piece of limestone. It is believed to have been constructed during the reign of pharaoh Khafre (2558–2532 BCE), whom historians believe is depicted in the statue's face. The Sphynx overlooks the Nile, and its immediate proximity to the Giza pyramids makes it the most prominent tourist attraction of a country filled with well-preserved ancient wonders. Guided tours, complete with transportation via camelback, are readily available to tourists, and at night a light show is projected onto the site as the Sphynx narrates the history of Egypt in a spectacular merging of ancient and modern artistry.

While in Khamoon, Lara also traverses around a giant obelisk as she attempts to access the Sanctuary of the Scion. Obelisks are geometric stone pillars that come to a point and are usually erected to honor a god or pharaoh, or commemorate an occasion. The word "obelisk" was coined by the ancient Greeks; they were originally called "tekhenu" by ancient Egyptians.

Incredibly, ancient obelisks were usually carved from a single piece of stone—predominantly red granite from the quarries at Aswan. While the transport of obelisks is well-documented in ancient Egyptian texts, the mechanics of raising them was not. This has inspired many archaeologists and engineers to muse over how it was done—and even attempt raising their own, to varying degrees of success. As with most of their ancient structures, the obelisk is a marvel of Egyptian engineering and art.

You may have seen ancient Egyptian obelisks around the world, in cities such as Paris, New York City, Istanbul, London, Rome, and more; some were gifted, and some were taken. The best way to see them is where they were intended: in Egypt, usually at the entrances to temples or in courtyards. With this in mind, a visit to the Karnak and Luxor Temple complexes are in order to view two such impressively intact obelisks.

VARYING LOCATIONS, EGYPT

In *Tomb Raider: The Last Revelation* (1999), Core Design chose to do away with globetrotting and focus on an epic adventure in Egypt. In the game, a young Lara explores the King's Valley, Karnak, Alexandria, and Cairo. *The Last Revelation* introduced—among other things—a rudimentary crafting system that allowed Lara to combine inventory items, as well as new items such as the crossbow, the ever-useful flashlight, and the ability to swing on ropes.

If you can manage a quick two-hour flight from Cairo to Luxor (known as Thebes to ancient Egyptians), it is well worth it. Once in Luxor, you will be overwhelmed with the sightseeing options available to you, all within close proximity to one another.

A great place to start are the massive temple complexes of Karnak and Luxor. The area surrounding them was a primary site of worship for the "Theban Triad" of gods—Amun, Mut, and Khansu. The Karnak complex was constructed over a period of nearly two thousand years. In it you will find massive pylons flanking doors to temples, courtyards, the famous Hypostyle Hall with over 130 massive columns, the aforementioned obelisks, and much more.

The younger Luxor Temple complex is located just over a mile away—the two were once connected by an avenue of over a thousand sphinx statues. The remnants of the "Avenue of the Sphinxes" welcomes you to Luxor Temple, after which you'll see several stunning courts; massive statues of Ramses II; individual chapels for Amun, Mut, and Khonsu; and even the remains of a Roman fort. You can easily spend an entire day wandering the two complexes.

When finished, you'll find another must-see just across the Nile. The Valley of the Kings is part of the Theban Necropolis and the burial site of many royal figures in Egyptian history. With over sixty tombs or burial chambers discovered so far, the site garnered massive international attention with the discovery of the tomb of Tutankhamun in the 1920s. While you will have to travel to the Egyptian Museum in Cairo to see the brilliant gold sarcophagus of King Tut, the Valley of the Kings offers a trip back in time with the incredibly well-preserved relief work and painted walls in the various chambers.

On the way back up north, we have one more suggestion. Although Lara has never been, visiting the Siwa Oasis in western Egypt is often overlooked but highly recommended. Featuring hundreds of fresh and saltwater springs with palm and olive trees peppered between them, both the water and the sand itself are lauded for natural healing. The remote town is also home to many ruins. The Mountain of the Dead, a hill featuring thousands of rock-cut tombs, is one of the most impressive.

If you want to round out Lara's list, a trip to Alexandria is also warranted. A port city north of Cairo, Alexandria sits on the Mediterranean and was once the site of the Great Library of Alexandria, another of the Seven Wonders of the Ancient World. Although none of the original library remains today, you can visit the Bibliotheca Alexandrina, which aims to capture the spirit of the original library through scholarship and shared knowledge. The city is also full of museums, plazas, and the beautiful Citadel of Qaitbay.

While traveling throughout Egypt it is suggested to dress modestly to protect yourself from the hot desert sun and to respect the practices of the Egyptian people. Women are not required to wear headscarves unless visiting specific religious sites like a mosque, but head coverings are incredibly helpful for avoiding painful sunburns. Another tip—in Egypt, weekends are Friday and Saturday, with the work week starting on Sunday. There will be less traffic on Friday with locals taking a day of rest, but most tourist attractions remain open.

GHANA

Lara pursues millionaire playboy antagonist James Rutland to Ghana in *Tomb Raider: Legend* (2006). After uncovering a ruin hidden behind a massive waterfall, Lara must defeat leopards and mercenaries alike before getting her hands on Rutland.

Ghana—formerly known as the Gold Coast for its primary export—sits in the Gulf of Guinea in West Africa. It was only in 1957 that four regions—the Gold Coast Crown Colony, the Ashanti Crown Colony, the Northern Territories of the Gold Coast, and the Trust Territory of Togoland—united under the Ghana Independence Act and became the Republic of Ghana.

In addition to gold, today Ghana is the second-largest producer of cocoa in the world. It has also become a tourism hub, featuring a diverse array of natural attractions, including dazzling beaches, sprawling national parks, and hiking trails through mountainous regions, among so much more.

As for exploring ruins, you will be hard-pressed to find any similar to those from *Tomb Raider: Legend* (2006) in Ghana, through which Lara pursues antagonist James Rutland to get his piece of the sword Excalibur. Rather, you can explore a variety of impressive forts, castles, and cathedrals, which are beautiful but have a dark past. They reflect European colonial history during the rush to stake a claim in the gold-rich land and participation in the Atlantic slave trade.

However, as with the rest of Africa, Ghana has a rich indigenous history worth exploring. The Ashanti Empire is of particular note in the region, which expanded outside of Ghana into the Ivory Coast and Togo. At its height in the eighteenth century, it was known for its extensive trade network, beautiful architecture, and military strength, having successfully fought off colonization by the British for over seven decades.

The capital of the Ashanti Empire is the city of Kumasi, now the second-largest metropolitan area after Ghana's capital, Accra. Excellent examples of Asante traditional buildings can be found just outside of Kumasi. A UNESCO World Heritage Site, these sacred shrines are believed to be the last remaining Ashanti Empire structures today. Made from mud, plaster, and wood and topped with thatched roofs, the structures were susceptible to time and weather. But they have since been restored to preserve their legacy. Usually laid out in a series of four buildings with a courtyard in the center, the buildings boasted ornate reliefs and geometric designs painted a rich orange color.

If you time things right, Kumasi is also home to one of Ghana's many traditional celebrations—the Adae Kese Festival. Tourists taking part in this celebration can expect to see colorful public displays by chiefs and queen mothers to honor the achievements of the Ashanti. The festivities are presided over by the modern-day Ashanti king, known as the Asantehene.

Thank you to our Africa travel guide and recipe consultants: *Meagan LaBrasseur; Maggie Elmanesterly; Fouad Adel; Owusu Dennis; Dane Wostenberg; Ahmad Alkaabi of Tomb Raider Arabia*

AFRICAN CUISINE
PLANTAIN CHIPS

| ◐ **LOCATION:** AFRICA | 🫙 **YIELD:** 4 SERVINGS | 🔥 **DIFFICULTY RATING:** 1 OUT OF 3 |

Frying is a common method of preparation for plantains. The bite-sized snack can be cut in many different ways, such as in cubes, thin or thick slices, or chips, making for a ready-to-travel sugar-powered energy booster, and a delicious one at that. The provided recipe will result in some delicious round chips.

🕑 **PREP TIME:** 10 MINUTES   🕑 **COOK TIME:** 10 MINUTES

TOOLS NEEDED: Mandolin or knife, Large bowl, Dutch oven or large heavy-bottomed pot, Kitchen thermometer, Slotted spoon

INGREDIENTS:

2 unripe (yellow-green) plantains

1 tablespoon kosher salt, divided

Vegetable oil for frying

DIRECTIONS:

1. Peel the plantains by cutting off both ends, slicing the peel lengthwise, and peeling it off.

2. Slice the plantains in thin rounds with a mandolin or a sharp knife.

3. Place the plantain slices and a teaspoon of salt in a bowl of water. Let soak while you heat a few inches of oil in a Dutch oven to 350°F.

4. Drain the plantain slices, and dry with a paper towel.

5. Place the plantains in the oil in batches (to avoid overcrowding), and fry for 4 minutes, or until golden brown and crisp, turning occasionally. Remove with a slotted spoon and place on a paper towel–lined plate to drain. Sprinkle with salt.

6. Repeat with the rest of the plantains, and enjoy once fully cooled and crisped.

EGYPTIAN CUISINE
KOFTA KEBAB

| **◑ LOCATION:** KHAMOON, EGYPT | **🍶 YIELD:** 8 KEBABS | **🔥 DIFFICULTY RATING:** 1 OUT OF 3 |

Kofta comprises a swath of meatball and meatloaf dishes from various countries, including the Middle East and Central Asia. It's one of many popular kebab preparations and is common among Egyptian restaurants.

RECIPE ORIGINS

Kofta kebabs originate from the Turkish "Şiş köfte." Turkish cuisine was heavily influenced by the Ottoman Empire (1299–1922 CE), a fusion of Asian, Armenian, Balkan, Eastern European, Mediterranean, and Middle Eastern cuisines. This explains why kofta kebabs are such a widespread tradition.

⏱ PREP TIME: 30 MINUTES   **⏱ COOK TIME:** 10 MINUTES   **⏱ INACTIVE TIME:** 30 MINUTES

TOOLS NEEDED: Bamboo skewers, Large bowl, Baking sheet or large plate, Grill

INGREDIENTS:

1 pound ground lamb

¼ cup yellow onion, minced

¼ cup chopped fresh parsley

1 tablespoon minced garlic (about 4 cloves)

1 teaspoon cumin

1 teaspoon kosher salt

½ teaspoon allspice

½ teaspoon coriander

¼ teaspoon smoked paprika

¼ teaspoon cardamom

¼ teaspoon cayenne pepper

¼ teaspoon black pepper

DIRECTIONS:

1. Soak the bamboo skewers in water for at least 30 minutes.

2. Place the ground lamb, onion, parsley, garlic, cumin, salt, allspice, coriander, paprika, cardamom, cayenne pepper, and black pepper into a large bowl, and mix with your hands until fully combined.

3. Divide the mix into 8 parts, forming large finger-length ovals, about 1-inch thick.

4. Place a bamboo stick through each meat patty, and place on a baking sheet or serving platter. Cover with plastic wrap, and refrigerate for 30 minutes. While the meat is in the refrigerator, preheat a grill to medium heat.

5. Place the kebabs on the grill for 6 to 8 minutes, turning every 3 minutes, until browned and the internal temperature has reached 160°F. If you don't have a grill, you can bake these at 425°F for 20 to 25 minutes.

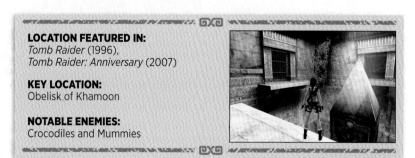

LOCATION FEATURED IN:
Tomb Raider (1996),
Tomb Raider: Anniversary (2007)

KEY LOCATION:
Obelisk of Khamoon

NOTABLE ENEMIES:
Crocodiles and Mummies

EGYPTIAN CUISINE
TA'AMIYA

| ⟨●⟩ **LOCATION:** UNDISCLOSED, EGYPT | 📋 **YIELD:** 16 BALLS (4 SERVINGS) | 🔥 **DIFFICULTY RATING:** 2 OUT OF 3

Deep-fried balls made from seasoned fava beans or chickpeas are a worldwide sensation. Known most commonly as "falafel," the dish is called "ta'amiya" in Egyptian Arabic and in Egyptian culture is traditionally prepared using fava beans. Ta'amiya is a favored street food and offers a vegetarian alternative to the Kofta Kebabs. Eat them on their own or place them in some pita bread with pickled vegetables, salad, and tahini sauce for a great sandwich.

RECIPE ORIGINS

Some historians believe falafel originated in Egypt, potentially thousands of years ago. However, oil for deep frying would have likely been too expensive in ancient Egypt, and the earliest written records of falafel date back to only the late nineteenth century. Several regions and cultures claim the popular dish as their own, leading to some contention around its creation, although it is safe to attribute it to the Middle East region.

🕐 **PREP TIME:** 6 HOURS　　　🕐 **COOK TIME:** 20 MINUTES

TOOLS NEEDED: Food processor or blender, Medium frying pan, Kitchen thermometer

INGREDIENTS:

2 cups dried split-shelled fava beans

1 tablespoon minced garlic (about 4 cloves)

1 large yellow onion, diced

2 tablespoons minced parsley

2 tablespoons tahini

2 tablespoons lemon juice

½ tablespoon olive oil

1 teaspoon cumin

1 teaspoon kosher salt

½ teaspoon black pepper

½ teaspoon paprika

Vegetable oil, for frying

DIRECTIONS:

1. Soak the fava beans in water overnight (or at least 6 hours), then rinse and drain.

2. Place the beans in a food processor or blender with the garlic, onion, parsley, tahini, lemon juice, oil, cumin, paprika, salt, and pepper. Process until a paste forms.

3. Form the paste into 16 golf ball–sized balls.

4. Place an inch of vegetable oil on the bottom of a medium frying pan. Bring it to 350°F over medium heat.

5. Fry a couple of the balls in the pan at a time, making sure not to overcrowd. Fry for 3 minutes on one side, then turn around and fry another 2 minutes. The balls should be golden brown.

6. Remove and let drain on a paper towel–lined plate.

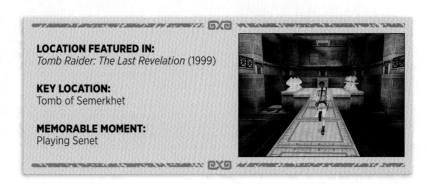

LOCATION FEATURED IN:
Tomb Raider: The Last Revelation (1999)

KEY LOCATION:
Tomb of Semerkhet

MEMORABLE MOMENT:
Playing Senet

GHANIAN CUISINE
JOLLOF

| **LOCATION:** UNDISCLOSED, GHANA | **YIELD:** 8 SERVINGS | **DIFFICULTY RATING:** 2 OUT OF 3 |

Jollof and its numerous regional variations are highly common throughout West Africa. Traditionally, it's made with long-grain rice, tomato paste, vegetables, and spices, and topped with grilled chicken, hard-boiled eggs, or any number of flavorful local meats. In Ghana, canned tomatoes and chicken bouillon cubes are more readily available, and any part of the chicken can be used to complete the meal.

RECIPE ORIGINS

Jollof originates from the West African Jollof Empire (1350–1549 CE). The popular dish has ignited a friendly rivalry, particularly among Nigeria and Ghana, commonly referred to as the Jollof Wars. Each country's method of cooking the dish vies to be recognized as superior, though this ranges from humorously (such as on social media) to violently and even to televised jollof cooking competitions.

PREP TIME: 10 MINUTES

COOK TIME: 65 MINUTES

TOOLS NEEDED: Dutch oven or large pot, Aluminum foil

INGREDIENTS:

3 tablespoons vegetable oil, divided

1 pound boneless, skinless chicken thighs, cut in 2-inch pieces

Salt and black pepper, to taste

2 yellow onions, minced, divided

1 (28-ounce) can whole plum tomatoes

6 cloves garlic

1 small chunk of ginger root (about 1 inch)

4 carrots, sliced into thin rounds (about 1 cup)

1 red bell pepper, diced

1 Scotch bonnet pepper (or habanero pepper), seeds and pith removed, minced

2 teaspoons curry powder

3 cups water

2 chicken bouillon cubes

3 tablespoons tomato paste

2 teaspoons thyme

2 bay leaves

2 cups basmati rice, rinsed

1 cup peas

DIRECTIONS:

1. Heat 1 tablespoon vegetable oil in your Dutch oven or large pot on medium-high, and cook your chicken thighs in the heated oil for 6 minutes, turning often, or until browned and fully cooked through. Season with salt and pepper while it's cooking. Set the chicken aside.

2. Blend together one of the minced onions, whole plum tomatoes, garlic, and ginger until it makes a smooth puree.

3. Heat the remaining 2 tablespoons of oil on medium-high in the Dutch oven, and then add the other minced onion, carrots, bell pepper, and Scotch bonnet pepper. Cook for 5 minutes, or until the veggies begin to soften. Add in the curry powder, and cook for 30 seconds more.

4. Add in the puree, water, bouillon cubes, tomato paste, thyme, bay leaves, 1 teaspoon salt, and ½ teaspoon black pepper. Bring to a simmer, then turn the heat to low and cook for 30 minutes, or until the liquid has reduced by half, stirring occasionally.

5. Mix in the rice and peas, bring back to a boil, and then reduce the heat to low. Cover the pot with aluminum foil and then the lid. Simmer for 20 minutes on low until the rice is fully cooked and the liquid is absorbed. Remove the bay leaves, fluff the rice with a fork, add the cooked chicken on top, and serve.

LOCATION FEATURED IN:
Tomb Raider: Legend (2006)

KEY LOCATION:
Amahlin

MEMORABLE MOMENT:
Revealing the ruins hidden behind the waterfall

TRAVEL TIPS & TRICKS

Before you set off on an international adventure, be sure to check our travel tips and tricks to get the most of your time abroad.

TRAVEL DOCUMENTATION

- **Passport:** Most countries require a passport for foreign entry. Ensure your passport hasn't expired before booking your trip—some countries require passports to be valid for at least six months after arrival.

- **Travel Visas:** Check to see if your destination(s) require a visa for entry and how the visa is granted. Some visas are granted upon arrival of the country after filling out an application and paying a fee. Others require applications at the nearest foreign consulate of the country you wish to visit.

HEALTH AND SAFETY

- **Government Travel Warnings:** Because the world's geopolitical landscape is constantly changing, it's important to check for travel warnings before you depart on an international trip. Most countries update their travel advisories daily and factor in everything from crime to disease and natural disasters.

- **Vaccinations:** Most of us are only vaccinated for diseases native to our country of residence. Before traveling internationally, call your doctor to find out if you need additional vaccines to protect you abroad.

- **Cultural Concerns:** Be sure to research any potential cultural concerns relevant to you before booking your trip. Factor in your gender, sexual orientation, race, and religion, and see if there are conflicting values in your destination.

- **Traveler's Insurance:** Traveler's insurance can be very important if you get sick or injured abroad. Check to see if your health insurance already has a travel insurance policy, or if you need to buy a specific plan for your destination.

- **Water Safety:** Research the water quality of where you are traveling. If it is a concern, stick to bottled water only, or invest in a reusable water bottle with an advanced filtration system for use on tap water.

- **Food Safety:** Be sure to research any food sensitivities or allergies you may have and keep a translation of it on you. Also, research if there are any regional dishes or types of food that are notoriously hard on visitors' stomachs.

PACKING:

- **Cut It in Half:** Lay out everything you want to take and then cut your selections in half. Do not forget to leave room (and weight) in your luggage for souvenirs!

- **Carry On:** Ensure you pack at least two days of essentials in your carry-on luggage in case your checked luggage is delayed or lost.

- **Backpacks:** If you're going to be on your feet for extended periods of time, backpacks are larger, safer, and less harmful to your back than shoulder purses or camera bags.

- **Luggage Scale:** Chances are you will return from a big trip with more items than you arrived with. To ensure you do not go over the weight limit for checked baggage, get a weight scale and be mindful of what you buy throughout your trip.

- **Electrical Adaptors and Converters:** Be sure to check the plug type and voltage of your destination country. The adaptors simply ensure your electronics can plug into the wall. Converters ensure the voltage of an outlet matches your devices. An incorrect voltage can result in damaging some electronics.

- **First Aid:** Pack some first aid basics such as generic pain relievers, bandages, antibacterial gel, moleskin, and sunscreen.

- **Medication:** Research if there are any restrictions on specific medications you are taking in your destination country, especially if they are injectable meds. Carry a doctor's note and proof of prescription on you at all times and leave medication in its original container. Never pack important medication in your checked bags, and to be extra safe, you can split your medication between your travel bag and your hotel upon arrival in case your property is lost or stolen.

- **Important Documents:** Ensure you have digital *and* physical copies of all important documents. This includes copies of your visa, passport, hotel and flight reservations, trip itinerary, personal contact information, the address of your country's embassy in the destination country, and any other essential information.

CURRENCY

- **Call Your Bank:** Be sure to call your bank or log a travel itinerary online before you depart. If you do not, many banks will decline charges to your debit or credit card, assuming they are fraudulent.

- **Currency Exchange:** If traveling to a country that uses a different currency, it is best to wait until arrival and take out cash via airport ATMs, especially if your card covers ATM charges. Some large hotel chains will also exchange popular world currencies at their reception.

- **Keep Small Bills:** Ensure you keep small bills on you for snacks and small purchases, or tipping, and quick cab rides when needed.

- **Payment Apps:** Investigate the most common payment methods in the country you are visiting prior to departure. Some countries like China are moving away from cash and card payments, instead using app-based QR code payments.

ARRIVAL & EXPLORATION:

- **Jet Lag:** If you are likely going to contend with severe jet lag, be prepared to push throughout it. Don't nap upon arrival, try to be active the day of your arrival and act as if you're already on local time.

- **Hotel Business Card:** If you expect communication to be an issue, grab a business card from the reception of your hotel so you can show it to taxi drivers and ensure an accurate drop-off.

- **Cell Plan:** Either opt for a local hotspot so you can use your phone on Wi-Fi, or ensure your phone plan covers the country you are traveling to so you aren't surprised with a massive phone bill upon return.

- **Look for Free Walking Tours:** Many popular tourist destinations have free walking tours available for visitors in an assortment of languages. This is a great first-day activity if you want to home in on the best sites to see during the rest of your trip.

- **Tourism Apps:** If you have a strong phone signal or a hotspot and your destination is walking-friendly, many cities have official tourism apps that use GPS to showcase landmarks near you or navigate you to a destination of your choice.

- **Investigate Transportation:** Figure out how you're going to get around before departure. While Uber and Lyft are popular internationally, some countries don't allow rideshare apps at all. Download important apps and set up profiles before your departure. If you plan on taking public transportation, be sure to research the routes you'll need to know.

CULTURE:

- **Learn Language Basics:** It is always best to learn basic phrases of the language in your destination country. Suggested terms include: "Hello," "please," "thank you," "you're welcome," "excuse me," "I'm sorry," and "I'm sorry, I don't speak [the language in question]."

- **Know Tipping Rules:** Know the rules of tipping before departure, and keep change available if needed. Some countries expect tips for a variety of services, while others consider tips insulting.

- **Research Local Faux Pas:** Research cultural faux pas in your destination country. For example, in many countries it is considered rude to point with your index finger.

- **Respect Religious Rules:** If you intend to visit sites of worship, ensure you are aware of the rules of dress and conduct before you leave your hotel.

- **Follow the Laws:** This may seem basic, but if you do not research common laws ahead of time, you may not realize you're breaking them. For example, chewing gum is banned in the immaculately clean city-state of Singapore.

RESPONSIBLE TOURISM:

- **Buy Local:** Whenever possible, support local artisans and vendors rather than big-box shops.

- **Tour Local:** Research local tour companies rather than booking through large international travel sites if possible. You'll be putting your money into the local economy.

- **Investigate Animal Tourism:** Close encounters with wildlife are a draw to many travelers, but research ahead of time to ensure that the animals you are interacting with are properly cared for.

- **Ask for Photos:** Be sure to ask permission to photograph people in local costume or dress, even if you suspect they are glad to pose for you.

TERMS & MEASUREMENT CONVERSIONS

KITCHEN MEASUREMENTS

CUP	TBSP	TSP	FL OZ
1/16 CUP	1 TBSP	3 TSP	1/2 FL OZ
1/8 CUP	2 TBSP	6 TSP	1 FL OZ
1/4 CUP	4 TBSP	12 TSP	2 FL OZ
1/3 CUP	5 1/3 TBSP	16 TSP	2 2/3 FL OZ
1/2 CUP	8 TBSP	24 TSP	4 FL OZ
2/3 CUP	10 2/3 TBSP	32 TSP	5 1/3 FL OZ
3/4 CUP	12 TBSP	36 TSP	6 FL OZ
1 CUP	16 TBSP	48 TSP	8 FL OZ

GALLON	QUART	PINT	CUP	FL OZ
1/16 GAL	1/4 QT	1/2 PINTS	1 CUP	8 FL OZ
1/8 GAL	1/2 QT	1 PINTS	2 CUP	16 FL OZ
1/4 GAL	1 QT	2 PINTS	4 CUP	32 FL OZ
1/2 GAL	2 QT	4 PINTS	8 CUP	64 FL OZ
1 GAL	4 QT	8 PINTS	16 CUP	128 FL OZ

WEIGHT

GRAMS	OUNCE
14 G	1/2 OZ
28 G	1 OZ
57 G	2 OZ
85 G	3 OZ
113 G	4 OZ
142 G	5 OZ
170 G	6 OZ
283 G	10 OZ
397 G	14 OZ
454 G	16 OZ
907 G	32 OZ

OVEN TEMPERATURES

CELSIUS	FAHRENHEIT
93°C	200°F
107°C	225°F
121°C	250°F
135°C	275°F
149°C	300°F
163°C	325°F
177°C	350°F
191°C	375°F
204°C	400°F
218°C	425°F
232°C	450°F

LENGTH

METRIC	2.5 CM	5 CM	10 CM	15 CM	20 CM	25 CM	30 CM
IMPERIAL	1 IN	2 IN	4 IN	6 IN	8 IN	10 IN	12 IN

INSIGHT EDITIONS

PO Box 3088
San Rafael, CA 94912
www.insighteditions.com

Find us on Facebook: www.facebook.com/InsightEditions
Follow us on Twitter: @insighteditions

CRYSTAL DYNAMICS

SQUARE ENIX

Publisher: Raoul Goff
VP of Licensing and Partnerships: Vanessa Lopez
VP of Creative: Chrissy Kwasnik
VP of Manufacturing: Alix Nicholaeff
Publishing Director: Mike Degler
Editorial Director: Vicki Jaeger
Editor: Anna Wostenberg
Senior Production Editor: Jennifer Bentham
Production Manager: Sam Taylor
Senior Production Manager, Subsidiary Rights: Lina s Palma

Props by Lara Croft Tonner Doll Passion (Christophe Croft & Fan Wapiti) & Xeno-Morpheus, David Paracuellos Gil & MaxTRS
Additional Screenshots by Raiding the Globe
Designed by Dan Caparo
Photography by Ted Thomas
Food & Prop Styling by Elena P. Craig

ROOTS of PEACE ● REPLANTED PAPER

Insight Editions, in association with Roots of Peace, will plant two trees for each tree used in the manufacturing of this book. Roots of Peace is an internationally renowned humanitarian organization dedicated to eradicating land mines worldwide and converting war-torn lands into productive farms and wildlife habitats. Roots of Peace will plant two million fruit and nut trees in Afghanistan and provide farmers there with the skills and support necessary for sustainable land use.

Manufactured in Turkey by Insight Editions

10 9 8 7 6 5 4 3 2 1